Plugged-in to the Dynamic Word

Living in Faith, Love, and Hope

Larry Grabill

BibleTheme Publications

Copyright© 2012 by Larry Grabill
All rights reserved

2nd edition published by BibleTheme Publications 09/2020
ISBN 978-0-9717235-4-2

1st edition published by WestBow Press 08/2012

All Scripture quotations, unless otherwise indicated, are taken from the New King James Version. Copyright© 1979, 1980, 1982 by Thomas Nelson, Inc. Used by permission. All rights reserved.

Contents

Chapter 1. Loss of Spiritual Dominion 11
Chapter 2. Triad of Spiritual Conquest 19
Chapter 3. The Capacities of the Heart 33
Chapter 4. The Nature of Truth 55
Chapter 5. Faith Restored 73
Chapter 6. Love Portrayed; Love Engaged 91
Chapter 7. Hope Fulfilled 111
Chapter 8. The Spiritual Dynamics of Attitude 135
Chapter 9. Fruit of the Spirit 149
Chapter 10. The Triads Blended Express Faith, Love, and Hope 155

Foreword

"Most churches claim to accept the Bible as their rule of faith and practice. However, one needs only to read and listen to find that often personal interpretation wins over letting the Word interpret itself. Various disciplines and theologians sometimes fall into a line of reasoning which seems to take away from the inspiration, infallibility, and inerrant teaching of the Bible in the original manuscripts.

"Brother Grabill has, we believe, attempted to let the Bible interpret itself. He has highlighted the triad of faith, love, and hope. In developing his thesis he has dared to give us the Bible's teaching from the Bible. In so doing he may frighten those whose allegiance is more to form than faith. Whether he has established his thesis completely will be the determination of those who seek to approve or disapprove it.

"All of us should be challenged by his insightful presentation. The book demands our careful study and a biblical response. It is high time that we once again become Biblicists even if it eventually demands a revision in the way we present the Bible's teachings. Grabill's emphasis on a conquering Church is a truth that needs to be reemphasized in our day when many are content to simply wait for the return of the Lord."

Omar Lee, D.Th., Retired Chairman of the Department of Theology, Kansas City College and Bible School.

Plugged-in to the Dynamic Word

Acknowledgements

For the 20 years that I have been developing the thoughts expressed in this book, many people have contributed. Evangelists Henry Lelear and Duane Smith were some of the first to encourage me with their interest in my work.

Dr. Ray Dunning, Dr. Elmer Colyer, Dr. David Gordeuk, Dr. Omar Lee, and Tom Ellis have been most helpful with their frank, constructive criticism.

My son, Pastor Stanley Grabill, has given me valuable input. What a spiritual blessing his unwavering dedication to Christ has been to me! My other three children—and the families of all four—have also been valuable sources of inspiration. I would be left with less confidence in the power of God's Word to make a difference in people's lives if I had not been able to witness that power in their lives.

Etim Uloh Edumoh, the president of Grace Bible Institute in Nigeria, has been a big influence. In our close working relationship we have developed a mutual concern for communicating biblical truths to his fellow Africans. This has become a large part of the incentive to write this book.

To all of these I say a big thank you!

My wife, Mary deserves recognition for putting up with my absentmindedness during the long periods of time I was so deeply lost in thought. I was miserable company. May the Lord bless her abundantly and have mercy on her husband.

Introduction

This book seeks to set forth the Bible's central theme and, within the frame of that key idea, portray one comprehensive picture of the whole of Scripture. This provides benefits that otherwise may not be gained:

- The ability to see each passage in its local context in relation to the larger central theme
- A better grasp of the Bible's thought pattern.
- The incentive to conquer the world in our personal lives and draw closer to God
- The knowledge to identify with Christ's operation to save the lost and conquer the kingdom of Satan

We demonstrate that the Bible's central theme, or key idea, can be defined as spiritual conquest through faith, love, and hope. We do this by attempting to overview the Bible through the periscope of this motif. In other words, we try the key in the lock to see if it works. In so doing, we see the Bible's passages coming to light and its basic parts coming together to compose a whole book. Thus our study confirms that our proposed central message, key idea, or motif is indeed the structural fabric of the Bible.

The Bible is interwoven with the threads of God-given faith, love, and hope. These dynamics of God's truth-program turn people from their self-centeredness to God-centeredness. Faith turns one from humanistic self-reliance to a healthy dependence on God. Love turns one from sensual selfishness to loving God, others, and to holding Christian values, with the key being an unselfish love. This love chooses the good and rejects evil. Hope turns a person from being earthly and materialistic to placing hope in spiritual values. Viewing the Bible through these concepts brings the whole of Scripture into focus.

Furthermore, faith, love, and hope are interactive. Faith prevails in its process of producing hope through the power of love; this produces a conquest mode. Yet this love-driven process cannot be humanly generated. It is a gift from God which applies His power to one's life.

This book is intended to saturate and quicken our hearts and minds with the various expressions of faith, love, and hope that we discover, and by this effect, powerfully motivate us to change the world for God. May we be lifted out of our spiritual slumber to march to the Spirit's drumbeat of victory and thus perpetuate a revival of holiness to the Lord.

Though this book is intended primarily for the general reader, we hope to establish that our study is a sound biblical work consistent with biblical theology's method of looking at the Bible.

What is biblical theology? John Bright explains that biblical theology "seeks to set forth in its own terms, and in its structural unity, the theology expressed in the Bible."[1]

Ray Dunning says, "There is coherence about the message of the total Scripture that makes it one book. It is one major task of biblical theology to attempt to identify this center and demonstrate how the various strands of biblical material implement this motif."[2]

Thus, in biblical theology, the passages of the Bible must be interpreted by its central theme or motif as it reflects the

---

[1] John Bright, *Authority of the Old Testament* (Grand Rapids: Twin Books, 1975)

[2] Ray Dunning, *Grace Faith and Holiness* (Kansas City: Beacon Hill Press, 1988), 35, 45.

overall context of Scripture. Of course this means that the central theme must be identified.

George Eldon Ladd, a recognized scholar of biblical theology, says, "Modern theology is quite unanimous in the opinion that the Kingdom of God was the central message of Jesus."[3] He also says that "the theology of the Kingdom of God is essentially one of conflict and conquest over the kingdom of Satan."[4]

---

[3] George Eldon Ladd, *A Theology of the New Testament* (Grand Rapids: William B. Eerdmans Publishing Co, 1993), 54.
[4] George Eldon Ladd, *A Theology of the New Testament*, 48.

Our stated definition of the Bible's central theme, spiritual conquest through faith, love, and hope, is consistent with Ladd's stated central message and theology of the kingdom. Ours goes one step further to address the all-important question of how conquest is accomplished.

The discipline of systematic theology develops from a different perspective than the perspective of biblical theology. Ray Dunning says, concerning systematic theology, "Its task is to bring the Christian faith into contact with the modern or contemporary situation.... Its function is to interpret Christian beliefs holistically in faithfulness to both the tradition and the present generation.... This characteristic suggests that systematic theology must operate between two poles.... What systematic theology properly does is stand in dynamic tension between the two."[5]

Accordingly, systematic theology is developed not only from the church's answers to questions that have arisen through time, but also from the Bible study and reasoning that is provoked by questions arising from contemporary needs and situations. Concerning biblical theology, it needs to be stated that the fact it is not called systematic does not mean it is without a system. It does systematically build conclusions. However, the organizing principle for biblical theology must be derived from the text of Scripture as expressed in the historical and cultural situation of the time.

Therefore, since we are endeavoring to do Bible study in a manner consistent with biblical theology's method of looking at

---

[5] *Grace Faith and Holiness,* 36, 37.

the Bible, we have identified our organizing principle: spiritual conquest through faith, love, and hope.

Through this motif we demonstrate the "structural unity" of the Bible, to use Ray Dunning's and John Bright's terminology. The significance of the faith-love-hope triad is that it focuses on God. Therefore, it makes people Godcentered as opposed to being self-centered. Thus selfcenteredness, the essence of sin, is overcome and spiritual conquest is achieved.

Much of this book involves a system of correlating the triad of faith, love, and hope to other biblical triads. In fact, the system is so neat that those who have never seriously studied the development of faith, love, and hope and their innerworking relation, may be inclined to judge that the system is being artificially imposed on Scripture. Therefore, let the reader allow, until he has thoroughly studied this book, that basic spiritual development could be a triune process, and that if it is it should not be surprising that a system of triads would be found in the Bible that reflects this pattern of development.

We seek to elucidate spiritual truth with illustrations from agriculture and simple physics. And this is scriptural, for Jesus repeatedly illustrated spiritual truths with natural concrete settings. By the way, this concrete-relational method of teaching is readily grasped by the learning styles of tribal cultures such as we find in Africa, and this gives them a cognitive advantage relative to spiritual truth.[6] Furthermore, it

---

[6] (see) David Hesselgrave, *Communicating Christ Cross-Culturally* (Grand Rapids: Zondervan Publishing House, 1991).

is an interesting possibility that God's spiritual laws and His natural laws have a common pattern at some level.

Plugged-in to the Dynamic Word

CHAPTER 1 Loss of Spiritual Dominion

A sailing vessel with properly adjusted rudder and sails can master the wind and waves to gain momentum and steer a course to its chosen destination, but without properly adjusted rudder and sails the ship will be inclined to toss about, wreck itself on the rocky coast, and sink.

When humans' sails of good conscience lost the winds of hope in God that had filled them and lost their faith-rudders of spiritual understanding, they were "at sea" as the saying goes. The result was that the ship of humanity sunk into the abyss of physical, spiritual and eternal death.

Animals are controlled by their instincts. In responding, therefore, to their appetites for food and the urges to mate, they fulfill God's purpose of keeping the earth replenished with their kind. God, however, has a higher purpose for people. [7] He wants them to experience dominion over His creation as His representatives. He wants them to know the thrill of realizing Him at work through them so they may experience or "prove what is that good and acceptable and perfect will of God" (Rom. 12:2). Therefore, God created man and woman in His own image. This gave them the faculties of intellect and conscience through which they are keenly

---

[7] "But man is utterly unlike any animal in other respects, and this is a fact that will not go away. It is the uniqueness of the human person that must be the starting point of a mature psychology, should such a discipline ever come into being," said Nobel prize-winning neurobiologist Sir John Eccles, and Daniel N. Robinson, *The Wonder of Being Human* (London: The Free Press, 1984), 150.

conscious of both the spiritual and the physical worlds and their power to make choices within these realms. In their God-image selfconscious minds, [8] God intended for men and women to be aware of their exalted position over the animals and their responsibility to subdue the animals (Gen. 1:26–27) along with their own animalistic drives and passions. When controlled by godly desires, these physical drives and emotional passions are good and beneficial. But without godly control, they work contrary to their intended purpose and make people dysfunctional.

By this consciousness of both the spiritual and the physical worlds, Adam and Eve were called to master the world, even though their world was not defective at that time. God intended the tension involved to keep them actively engaged in the healthy exercise of their powers. Therefore, a form of mastery over nature was God's basic agenda for humans from the start. Humanity, under the authority of God and blessed with spiritual gifts, exercised authority over its perfect world. This was the very world that later became the defective world as seen in John 14:30 and 1 John 2:15–16.

By this consciousness of both the spiritual and the physical worlds, Adam and Eve were called to master the world, even though their world was not defective at that time. God intended the tension involved to keep them actively engaged in the healthy exercise of their powers. Therefore, a form of mastery over nature was God's basic agenda for humans from

---

[8] "It is proposed to use the term 'self-conscious mind' for the highest of mental experiences. It implies knowing that one knows, which is of course initially a subjective or introspective criterion,' according to Sir John Eccles and Daniel N. Robinson, *The Wonder of Being Human* (London: The Free Press, 1984), 25.

the start. Humanity, under the authority of God and blessed with spiritual gifts, exercised authority over its perfect world.

This was the very world that later became the defective world as seen in John 14:30 and 1 John 2:15–16.

Being God Centered

Thus God created people not only as living biological organisms but also as spiritual beings. When God breathed into Adam the breath of life, his physical form received the "inner man" (Eph. 3:16) of heart, mind, and entire soul. Eve was created with the same physical and spiritual essence. Therefore, it was through the consciousness of their inner beings that Adam and Eve were in constant apprehension of God and His will. Their whole personalities were oriented to God, and through this relationship God controlled the earth. It is important to observe that this relationship was maintained through faith, love, and hope.

Faith in God kept them from eating of the Tree of the Knowledge of Good and Evil, for their faith included the spiritual understanding that God knew what was good for their personal well-being and their relationship to Him. To eat of the tree would have indicated that they felt the need to learn how to discern good and evil apart from God's revealed judgment. By not eating of the tree, they testified to their understanding that only God had the knowledge and moral character necessary to unfailingly judge what was good for them and what was evil (bad) for them. They could safely partake of the knowledge of good and evil only through God's revelation.

Love for God maintained in them the desire to be in constant communion with Him. This communion maintained and constantly nurtured the love of God in their hearts. This godly love caused them to love what God loved, namely the truth. They had "the love of the truth," (2 Thess. 2:10). They thus were inclined to love truth and hate falsehood. Consequently, they did not love the forbidden tree or the false way of eating its fruit. As we shall see, truth is God's prescribed program for us, and anything contrary to this and the agenda it entails is falsehood.

Hope in God was continual, because the faith of Adam and Eve was strong. Faith is the substance of hope (see Hebrews 11:1). This hope was the confidence that they, with all that the garden could afford, would live life to the fullest in open, constant communion with God forever. In God they were satisfied and fulfilled, needing no other hope.

The Subtle Coup

Satan was keenly aware of the power of God's spiritual dynamics for keeping people God-centered. Therefore, he devised a subtle plan to counteract their faith, love, and hope so that he could distract them from God.

As indicated, Eve lived by trusting God's judgment for determining what was good and what was evil. Whatever God said was good, she believed was good for her. Whatever He said was evil, she believed was harmful to her. Therefore, she was not interested in leaning to her "own understanding"

(Prov. 3:5) to determine what was good for her and what was bad for her.

But the serpent got her attention with his sensual and commanding presence. He brazenly suggested, contrary to God's word, that she would not die from eating of the fruit of the tree and that it would make her exceedingly wise (see Genesis 3:4–5). When Eve turned her attention from God to Satan, she made her fatal mistake for she was totally naive concerning evil. Formerly, her naiveté had been protected by her trust in God, but when she turned her attention away from God to Satan she was helplessly vulnerable. Thus Satan deceived Eve into believing that God might not have been representing the truth accurately.

She began to believe that the real reason God had kept Adam and her from eating of the Tree of the Knowledge of Good and Evil may have been to keep them hopelessly under His control by keeping them ignorant. God had said they would die if they ate of the fruit, but now she self-confidently doubted that they would "surely die" (Gen. 3:4), believing the serpent who was contradicting God's directive.

Eve began to consider good and evil, right and wrong, through naive pride in her own judgment that doubted God. This led to disastrous disobedience. In eating from the tree, Adam and Eve partook of false knowledge concerning what was good and evil. This knowledge circumvented the instruction God had given them and it left them void of the "knowledge of the truth" (1 Tim. 2:4). As a result, they were left in spiritual, moral, and intellectual confusion.

They also received the punishment of death that God had promised. No wonder they began to sense that they were naked, not only naked and devoid of physical covering but also devoid of spiritual life and much of the higher level of consciousness with which they were created. The loss of this consciousness, or spiritual understanding, was both the loss of their clear knowledge of God's will—a breakdown of the intellect—and of much of their instinctive sense of value—a breakdown of the conscience. This, in turn, also weakened their power to choose to do right—a breakdown of the will. Furthermore, Adam and Eve would continue to suffer the gradual breakdown of these faculties, at least for a time.

The fallout from Adam's sin did not affect just him, for every descendant inherited the lost of dominion Adam had maintained through constant, open communion with God. Thus "in Adam all die" (1 Cor. 15:22). This means that everyone is left to the depravity of heart caused by the lack of an intimate relationship with God. In essence, things fell apart because every person turned to following his own satanicallyinfluenced agenda rather than God's agenda. Furthermore, they lost spiritual dominance over their own animalistic drives and passions, which abandoned them to a floundering independence. Also, God lost His chosen means of control and dominion of the world (control through righteous people). Therefore, He would leave the rule of the earth largely to the laws of nature, including the impaired human nature, and the "god of this age," mentioned in 2 Corinthians 4:4. Of course God was still God and He had a plan for humans to regain dominance over their lives and conquer evil in the world. God would maintain the control necessary to keep Satan from defeating His ultimate purpose until righteous people could again exercise dominion over the world.

In this self-imposed curse, humans lost their spiritual dominion over their physical drives and passions, and this was mirrored in the loss of much of their dominion over the animals which had the counterparts of such passions. The curse subjected people to the serpent's bite and to the carnivorousness that came to other animals, but this curse also subjected humans to their own savage passions that resulted from their loss of relationship with God. Thus, people were destined to live in a world that consisted of nature taking its course under the dominion of Satan after the coming of sin. This is "the world" as we see it in the context of 1 John 2:16.

Some view "the world" of this context as primarily a spiritual system, but this is confusing. This world has spiritual connotations (evil spiritual connotations) because Satan, who is a spirit, has been given restricted dominion over it; but it is essentially a materialistic system. For this reason those who are "of the world," as opposed to those who are "not of this world" (John 15:19; 17:14), are unspiritual, earthly, and materialistic. They need to be born of the Spirit into spiritual life (John 3:5–6) to conquer their materialistic, earthly preoccupation. It needs to be emphasized that Satan's dominion was limited. God would allow him only so much liberty, as seen in Satan's acts against Job (Job 1:12). God still had general control of the universe and could break into the course of nature and its historical development at any time.

After the fall, people continued to deteriorate until they became wild, governed primarily by their unholy passions. The animals also progressed in their savagery because of the world's loss of God-dominion. Satan gladly drove this deterioration, because the more he could get people to submit to their evil passions, the more he could control them through those passions. Thus he became master of the world by enslaving the very beings who had originally been given dominion over the world. People would soon discover that Satan did not respect their dignity as God had. He did not have any concern for their welfare; his only purpose was to use them for his selfish ends.

All would have been lost had God not foreseen what was going to happen and planned a strategy for the survival of His kingdom and His people; namely, a strategy to eventually recapture and renovate the world. Understanding this strategy will plug us into God's plan to conquer Satan's control of individual lives and the world at large.

CHAPTER 2 Triad of Spiritual Conquest

Workers raised the sunken freighter, Al Kuwait, in the freshwater harbor of Kuwait by pumping many expanded polystyrene pellets down into the hall of the ship. The collective buoyancy of the many expanded pellets raised the vessel. Likewise, God had a plan to lift humanity which He was ready to put in play after the Edenic fall. He would insert the buoyancy of salvation, person by person, into the sunken ship of humanity, and by this act, eventually free creation from the bondage of sin's corruption (see Romans 8:21). By the collective buoyancy of many people living for God, this ship would rise to a level of being a formidable influence for godliness in the current society. The godly ones would not only realize salvation from eternally damnation, they would also effectively master the sea of life to advance the Kingdom of God against the kingdom of Satan.

A path can be traced by which God led people for strategic spiritual conquest. This involved a long process and eventually led to the point that God had everything in readiness to "anoint the Most Holy" (Dan. 9:24). The "Most Holy" was the Savior who would come to earth to provide the ultimate remedy for sin so that people could obtain the faith, love, and hope that would eventually restore God's dominion of the world.

However, before tracing this path certain things must be kept in mind. God really does work through faith, love, and hope to accomplish spiritual conquest. Eleven passages in the

New Testament Epistles mention faith, love, and hope and show their functions in interactive relationship with each other. These passages lay the foundation for establishing the premise that the dynamic process by which the Holy Spirit equips people to be spiritual conquerors is love with faith and hope incorporated. This is God's part in spiritual conquest—causing this triad to act in people. It is God's process of sanctification that cleanses hearts from sinful tendencies.

These passages also set the stage for establishing another premise, that basic Christian exercise is faith-prevailing in its process of producing hope through love. This is the triad being acted out by people toward God and others. It involves the part people play in spiritual conquest for society.

Brief definitions of faith, love, and hope will help establish a foundation for this study:

Faith is developing belief in God formed in the intellect that matures into the choice of the will to trust in God. It is God-reliance as opposed to the kind of self-reliance that diminishes or excludes trust in God.

Love, referring to the love of God, is distinguishable from mere human love. It is God's nature made known in Christ to us by which we love what God loves and hate what He hates. Thus we determine to act in character with God's will.

Hope is faith having laid hold of a specific promise of God. Or, stated another way, it is faith trusting God to fulfill a specific promise that He has made. It is also an appraisal of value in God, formed in the conscience, deeming God desirable and trustworthy.

With these definitions in mind, we proceed to Scriptures that show faith, love, and hope in interactive relationship with each other.

Faith, Love, and Hope in Romans 5:1–5

> Therefore, having been justified by faith, we have peace with God through our Lord Jesus Christ, through whom also we have access by faith into this grace in which we stand, and rejoice in hope of the glory of God. And not only that, but we also glory in tribulations, knowing that tribulation produces perseverance; and perseverance, character; and character, hope. Now hope does not disappoint, because the love of God has been poured out in our hearts by the Holy Spirit who was given to us.

Through faith by grace we are justified and have peace with God though Jesus. This means that we stand justified in God's sight as though we had never sinned. Through Jesus we also access the grace that enables us to stand and rejoice in hope. What is this particular hope? It is the glory of God, the glory that Jesus obtained in His victory over sin and Satan on the cross. It is this glory that provides the grace of justification and the grace to maintain victory over sin. This hope of the glory of God is faith having laid hold of the promise of victory over sin and spiritual defeat. We don't have to live in spiritual defeat.

But victorious living provokes tribulation from those who do not hope in the glory of God. Yet this tribulation produces perseverance which builds Christian character by drawing on the exercise of more faith, which produces more hope. And this hope does not disappoint us, because it is based on the promises of God who always delivers what He has promised.

Love is the power source for this process. The love of God, having been poured out in our hearts, enables us to endure the tribulation that produces this hope so that hope does not break down in the process of being built up. Faith is continually in the process of producing more hope through the power of love.

Faith, Love, and Hope in 1 Corinthians 13:4 and 13:13

> Love suffers long and is kind; love does not envy; love does not parade itself, is not puffed up; does not behave rudely, does not seek its own, is not provoked, thinks no evil; does not rejoice in iniquity, but rejoices in the truth; bears all things, believes all things, hopes all things, endures all things (13:4).
>
> And now abide faith, hope, love, these three; but the greatest of these is love" (13:13).

Obviously faith, love, and hope are all basic to Christian development and fruit-bearing. Yet love is the greatest of the three. Why? Because not only does love "love," but love also believes and hopes. Only through love can we actually have the necessary faith to believe and the necessary hope to endure the trials of life. Love, in itself, includes the processes of believing and hoping.

Many interpret "believe all things" to mean that love tries to believe good about everyone. Love certainly doesn't rejoice when iniquity is discovered in someone, yet love doesn't try to deceive itself in order to see good in people because love also rejoices in the truth. It is quite obvious that this Scripture is intended to convey that love rejoices in righteousness as opposed to iniquity because righteousness is important to God.

Faith, Love, and Hope in Galatians 5:5–6

> For we through the Spirit eagerly wait for the hope of righteousness by faith. For in Christ Jesus neither circumcision nor uncircumcision avails anything, but faith working through love.

To "wait for the hope of righteousness by faith" is to recognize that hope is yet to be fulfilled. When one comes into possession of the object of his hope, his hope is no longer hope because it is fulfilled. However, it is implied that faith working through love is the only exercise that "avails" for producing hope. Therefore, we see that faith prevails in its process of producing hope through the power of love even though it must wait for hope to be fulfilled. Faith prevails in its process of producing hope through love.

Faith, Love, and Hope in Ephesians 1:15–19

> Therefore I also, after I heard of your faith in the Lord Jesus and your love for all the saints, do not cease to give thanks for you, making mention of you in my prayers: that the God of our Lord Jesus Christ, the Father of glory, may give to you the spirit of wisdom and revelation in the knowledge of Him, the eyes of your understanding being enlightened; that you may know what is the hope of His calling, what are the riches of the glory of His inheritance in the saints, and what is the exceeding greatness of His power toward us who believe, according to the working of His mighty power.

Prior to this passage, Paul stated in verse 4 that the Ephesians were chosen "to be holy and without blame before Him in love." He was saying that this could happen only in the dynamic of love. Now he indicates that faith and love are qualities worthy of commendation and thanks to God. He sees in these dynamics the grounds for expecting the Ephesians to fulfill the hope of God's calling—this hope that is made possible through the "riches of His glory" and the "greatness of His power" that is the call to holiness of verse 4. Therefore, faith and love fulfill the hope that consists of experiencing holiness. From the other Epistles we know that faith works through love to accomplish this. So faith works through love to fulfill the hope of experiencing holiness.

Faith, Love, and Hope in Colossians 1:3–6

> We give thanks to the God and Father of our Lord Jesus Christ, praying always for you, since we heard of your faith in Christ Jesus and of your love for all the saints; because of the hope which is laid up for you in heaven, of which you heard before in the word of the truth of the gospel, which has come to you, as it has also in all the world, and is bringing forth fruit, as it is also among you since the day you heard and knew the grace of God in truth.

Paul gives thanks for the Colossians' "faith in Christ Jesus" and "love for all the saints" which has been perpetuated by their heavenly hope. Here we see hope building faith and love. After faith has produced hope through love, hope in turn produces more faith and love. Hope builds up faith and love, and this is evidence that the three build up each other.

Faith, Love, and Hope in 1 Thessalonians. 1:2–4

> We give thanks to God always for you all, making mention of you in our prayers, remembering without ceasing your work of faith, labor of love, and patience of hope in our Lord Jesus Christ in the sight of our God and Father, knowing, beloved brethren, your election by God.

Here faith, love, and hope are cited as evidence of being elected by God. By these qualities, the Thessalonians are recognized as God's chosen. Thus this passage highlights the three basic Christian elements of our study and portrays them as dynamic processes in that faith works, love labors, and hope exercises patience. Faith, love, and hope are these dynamic processes.

Faith, Love, and Hope in 1 Thessalonians. 5:8–10

> But let us who are of the day be sober, putting on the breastplate of faith and love, and as a helmet the hope of salvation. For God did not appoint us to wrath, but to obtain salvation through our Lord Jesus Christ, who died for us, that whether we wake or sleep, we should live together with Him.

This passage shows us that faith, love, and hope act as armor. The inference is that these protect us from spiritual defeat and therefore are necessary for spiritual battle and conquest. Faith, love, and hope act as spiritual armor to protect the Christian from spiritual defeat.

Faith, Love, and Hope in Hebrews 6:10–12

> For God is not unjust to forget your work and labor of love which you have shown toward His name, in that you have ministered to the saints, and do minister. And we desire that each one of you show the same diligence to the full assurance of hope until the end, that you do not become sluggish, but imitate those who through faith and patience inherit the promises.

The writer of Hebrews desires that the recipients of his letter conquer more spiritual territory by the same love-labor that compelled them to minister to the saints. They are not to be satisfied with shallow Christianity; they are to inherit all that God has promised them. By this love-labor they are to inherit the hope of these promises through faith. Therefore, hope is faith having laid hold of a specific promise of God through the power of love. In this case, the promise was the perfection that they were expected "to inherit." Hope is faith having laid hold of a specific promise of God through the power of love.

Faith, Love, and Hope in Hebrews 10:19–25

> Therefore, brethren, having boldness to enter the Holiest by the blood of Jesus, by a new and living way which He consecrated for us, through the veil, that is, His flesh, and having a High Priest over the house of God, let us draw near with a true heart in full assurance of faith, having our hearts sprinkled from an evil conscience and our bodies washed with pure water. Let us hold fast the confession of our hope without wavering, for He who promised is faithful. And let us consider one another in order to stir up love and good works, not forsaking the assembling of ourselves together, as is the manner of some, but exhorting one another, and so much the more as you see the Day approaching.

The epistle to the Hebrews relates the three dynamic elements of our study to each other in teaching how to conquer spiritually. A little concentration is required to grasp the connected message which draws one to boldly enter "the Holiest." "The Holiest" alludes to the Old Testament priest entering the inner, holiest room of the tabernacle. This is illustrative of entering complete, or entire, sanctification, a point of having ceased one's own works or agenda (see Hebrews 4:10) in favor of a "rest" of faith in God (Heb. 4:9). In this surrender to God, one becomes sanctified "completely" or entirely (see 1 Thessalonians 5:23) in the sense that no willful or voluntary resistance to God remains.

But to be a candidate for this sanctification by faith, one must have had his heart "sprinkled from an evil conscience," a conscience that is programmed to do evil and is guilty of sin. "Sprinkled" alludes to the priest sprinkling blood as a cleansing act before he enters the Holiest. Accordingly, to be ready for entire sanctification, one must have repented of his sinfulness so that his conscience is cleansed of guilt and programmed for righteousness. As one repents, he is forgiven, or "washed with pure water." This washing alludes to the tabernacle washing that typifies the cleansing of forgiveness.

Thus, having met the requirements and having entered a life of entire sanctification by faith, Christians must "hold fast the confession of their hope without wavering"—the hope that is a life victorious over sin. To help with this process, they should assemble together to stir up love with good works among one another. At the very least, this passage shows that faith, love, and hope work together to provide the boldness and confidence to enter, maintain and develop a life of complete or entire sanctification, "the new and living way" that God provides.

Faith, love, and hope work together to provide the boldness and confidence to enter, maintain, and develop a life of entire sanctification.

Faith, Love, and Hope in 1 Peter 1:3–9

> Blessed be the God and Father of our Lord Jesus Christ, who according to His abundant mercy has begotten us again to a living hope through the resurrection of Jesus Christ from the dead, to an inheritance incorruptible and undefiled and that does not fade away, reserved in heaven for you, who are kept by the power of God through faith for salvation ready to be revealed in the last time. In this you greatly rejoice, though now for a little while, if need be, you have been grieved by various trials, that the genuineness of your faith, being much more precious than gold that perishes, though it is tested by fire, may be found to praise, honor, and glory at the revelation of Jesus Christ, whom having not seen you love. Though now you do not see Him, yet believing, you rejoice with joy inexpressible and full of glory, receiving the end of your faith—the salvation of your souls.

God's people have been born a second time, and through this second birth they have received spiritual life—"a living hope." This hope-filled life consists of a genuine faith that will be tested through "various trials." This faith connects them to the power of God and causes them to love God and rejoice in Him even though they have not seen Him. This shows us that hope and faith build up love.

Faith, Love, and Hope in 1 Peter 1:20–23

> He indeed was foreordained before the foundation of the world, but was manifest in these last times for you who through Him believe in God, who raised Him from the dead and gave Him glory, so that your faith and hope are in God. Since you have purified your souls in obeying the truth through the Spirit in sincere love of the brethren, love one another fervently with a pure heart, having been born again, not of corruptible seed but incorruptible, through the word of God which lives and abides forever.

Two important factors command our attention in this letter. First, the recipients of Peter's letter have faith and hope in God as a result of having their souls purified through their obedience to the truth. This faith and this hope happen in love. Love's determination to act in character with God's will motivated them to obey the truth, and this developed a mature faith and hope. Love, with faith and hope incorporated, was acting in a sanctifying way. Second, they were to love each other with this same kind of pure, unselfish love.

At first thought, the phrase "love of the brethren" might appear to be only love existing between brethren. However, if this is what is meant, Peter would be saying since you love the brethren, love one another. This would be circular reasoning because "the brethren" and "one another" are the same people.

This would not be an intelligent statement on Peter's part. However, if we understand Peter to be referring to the love that the brethren (Christians) possess (the love of God), the meaning becomes clear.

In this light, he means: "Since you have purified your souls in obeying the truth through the Spirit in sincere love," it shows that you have the love of God. Therefore, love one another with this love. First, the love of God incorporating faith and hope sanctifies; second, it is pure unselfish love for others.

Therefore we can see that:
1. Faith is continually in the process of producing more hope through the power of love (see Romans and Galatians).
2. Love in itself includes the processes of believing and hoping (see 1 Corinthians 13).
3. Faith prevails in its process of producing hope through love (see Galatians).
4. Faith works through love to fulfill the hope of experiencing holiness (see Ephesians).
5. Hope builds up faith and love—evidence that the three build up each other (see Colossians).
6. Faith, love, and hope are dynamic processes and act as spiritual armor to protect us from defeat (see 1 Thessalonians).
7. Hope is faith having laid hold of a specific promise of God through the power of love (see Hebrews).
8. Faith, love, and hope work together to provide the boldness and confidence to enter, maintain, and develop a life of entire sanctification (see Hebrews).
9. Faith and hope build up love, giving more evidence that the three build up each other (as seen in 1 Peter).

10. Love incorporating faith and hope sanctifies and brings pure unselfish love for others (as seen in 1 Peter).

Summary

Generally we see that faith, love, and hope interactively build up each other in Christians while advancing them toward God-centeredness and holiness to conquer evil—love being the driving force in this conquest. Thus we can begin to comprehend that the dynamic process by which the Holy Spirit equips people to be spiritual conquerors is love with faith and hope incorporated, and that basic Christian exercise is faith prevailing in its process of producing hope through love.

The call for conquest through faith, love, and hope is the basic thrust of the Bible. We could say that the central motif of God's word is *spiritual conquest through faith, love, and hope*. We will get an overview of the Bible that brings the whole into focus when we look through this motif as our periscope. Then through that vision, as our minds plug-in into dynamic contact with the motif, our hearts will become interfaced with faith, love, and hope. And from this triad will come passionate desire to do God's will and champion His cause.

In our Bible study, we don't want to just satisfy our curiosity or to be fascinated with its uniqueness. We want to embrace the Word so that it grows in our hearts (see Acts 12:24) and lends us its spiritual power. Oh the joy of feeling the Word throbbing in my heart and setting it aflame for God!

Faith, love, and hope can each be viewed as one of three dynamic elements of a triad. These elements can each be correlated with one of the three dynamic elements of other triads and identified. We can therefore trace the application of faith, love, and hope through the Bible.

Plugged-in to the Dynamic Word

CHAPTER 3 The Capacities of the Heart

For a ship to effectively ply the waters and do battle in the name of its country, the hearts of its sailors must be vibrant, determined, and committed to their mission. We need vibrant, committed hearts full of godly love to masterfully navigate the rough waters we encounter in the service of our Lord. The Lord has a plan to condition our hearts for this. We have already established that God works through faith, love, and hope to accomplish His spiritual objectives. Now we need to ascertain how these dynamics condition our hearts and function in our lives.

The comforting reality is that Adam and Eve's choice to sin did not take God by surprise. God knew that sin would come into the world and He had a plan in mind to save people from it. The story of the Bible is the story of God putting this plan into action—His plan to conquer sin. George Eldon Ladd says, "It is the obvious intent of the Bible to tell a story about God and his acts in history for humanity's salvation."[9]

A dynamic process is involved, both the dynamic process through which God gives salvation and the process by which He enables people to "work out" their salvation (see Philippians 2:12). Salvation is received by faith. From that point on, all that is received from God comes through faith

---

[9] Ladd, *A Theology of the New Testament* (Grand Rapids: Wm. B. Eerdmans Publishing Co, 1993), 20.

(see Ephesians 2:8). Salvation cannot be earned. However, from the time salvation is received, it dynamically affects the

---

inner person to the effect of producing works of righteousness, or righteous acts. This is accomplished through love and hope as well as faith.

Therefore, "God's acts in history for humanity's salvation," in Ladd's words, constitute acts of imparting faith, love, and hope to hearts. God acts to enable people to exercise faith-prevailing-in-hope-through-love.

Why would we be interested in how these acts affect the heart? Because the heart is considered to be the seat of the depravity that has come to people from the Edenic fall. It is the central focus of God's efforts to restore righteousness to humankind. Jesus describes the heart in the parable of the four different soils.

From everyday life, this parable gives a graphic, earthly picture of the nature of the heart. All cultures of the world can relate to this concrete picture. People everywhere understand the process of seeds being sown and germinating into plants, and those plants producing fruit. This parable is recorded in Matthew 13:3–9 and the interpretation is given later in the chapter:

> Therefore hear the parable of the sower. When anyone hears the word of the kingdom, and does not understand it, then the wicked one comes and snatches away what was sown in his heart. This is he who received seed by the wayside. But he who received the seed on stony places, this is he who hears the word and immediately receives it with joy; yet he has no root in himself, but endures only for a while. For when tribulation or persecution arises because of the word, immediately he stumbles. Now he who received seed

The Capacities of the Heart

among the thorns is he who hears the word, and the cares of this world and the deceitfulness of riches choke the word, and he becomes unfruitful. But he who received seed on the good ground is he who hears the word and understands it, who indeed bears fruit and produces: some a hundredfold, some sixty, some thirty (Matt. 13:18–23).

In this parable, three different soils did not produce fruit. Jesus shows us that these soils represent the heart. The unproductive soils represent three different capacities of the heart.

The Different Soils

The first heart soil, the wayside heart, does not understand, implying that the heart is intended to have capacity for understanding spiritual matters even though this one doesn't. Therefore, the wayside soil is an illustration of deficient understanding relative to knowing and serving God. The understanding that can be received from God is a spiritual understanding that goes beyond natural, rational, cognitive processes, but it certainly involves reason.

The second heart soil, the stony heart, receives the "word" with joy, but "tribulation or persecution" causes it to stumble spiritually, showing that it is not really strong in its determination to serve God. This ability to make a choice and stick by it needs to be strengthened with more determination when a person desires to follow God. It implies that the heart has volitional capacity. Therefore, the stony soil is an illustration of the weak exercise of volition relative to right and wrong, good and evil.

The third heart soil, the thorny heart, also receives the word, but "the cares of this world and the deceitfulness of riches choke the word." Choked by the "deceitfulness of riches" implies seeking fulfillment in material things. This heart is taken up with material things. Its capacity for instinctively judging value only in terms of what one should be fervent and zealous about needs to place more value in God. Therefore, the thorny soil is an illustration of defective instinctive valuejudgments relative to the value of God and His will.

Many Scriptures ascribe understanding, volition, and instinctive value-judgment, or discernment, to the heart. Here are a few:

For Understanding:
1 Kings 3:9, 1 Kings 3:12, 1 Kings 4:29, Job 17:4, Job 38:36, Psalm 119:34, Proverbs 2:2, Proverbs 3:5, Proverbs
8:5, Proverbs 14:33, Proverbs 15:14, Mark 8:17, Ephesians 4:18

For Volition:
Exodus 25:2, 2 Chronicles 29:31, Matthew 18:35, Matthew 22:37, Acts 11:23, Romans 6:17, Romans 10:10, 1 Corinthians 7:37, 2 Corinthians 9:7, Ephesians 6:6, Hebrews 3:10, Hebrews 4:12

For Value Judgment:
Deuteronomy 8:5, Proverbs 3:3, Proverbs 10:8, Ecclesiastes 7:25, Ecclesiastes 8:16, Ecclesiastes 9:1,

---

Ecclesiastes 11:9, Isaiah 9:9, Isaiah 42:25, Isaiah 44:19, Isaiah 51:7, Jeremiah 24:7, Matthew 6:21

The Capacities of the Heart

Webster's and Mosby's dictionaries show that the capacities of understanding, volition, and value-judgment are identified with the intellect, the will, and the conscience, respectively, in the English worldview.

Intellect is the power and ability of the mind for knowing and understanding, as contrasted with feeling or with willing. According to *Mosby's Medical, Nursing and Allied Health Dictionary*,

> ...the will is the mental faculty that enables one to consciously choose or decide on a course of action. It is the act or process of exercising the power of choice. It is a wish, a desire or a deliberate intention. The will is a disposition or attitude toward another or others. It is determination or purpose.[10]

The conscience, according to Webster, is the inner sense of what is right or wrong in one's conduct or motives, impelling one toward right action. It means to follow the dictates of conscience.[11]

Since the Bible ascribes these capacities of understanding, volition and instinctive value-judgment to the heart, it follows that the faculties having these capacities are faculties of the heart. The idea of the conscience was included in the Hebrew

---

[10] *Mosby's Medical, Nursing, and Allied Health Dictionary*, 4th Edition, (Mosby-Year Book Inc.)

[11] *Random House Webster's Electronic Dictionary & Thesaurus,* College Edition, (WordPerfect Corporation, 1994).

word *leb* for the heart in the Old Testament.[12] This further establishes that the conscience is a faculty of the heart.

The Bible does not name a faculty that can be identified as the intellect, nor one that can be identified as the will (even though verses such as Romans 7:19, "For the good that I will to do, I do not do," come close). Yet we choose to use the words "intellect" and "will" because these words denote the faculties that the English worldview recognizes to have the Bible-described capacities of understanding and volition.

We need to treat the conscience more in depth than the dictionary treats it because the Bible does name this faculty and shows it in various contexts that the dictionary definition does not cover. The Bible portrays the conscience as capable of value-judgment. The consciences of the scribes and Pharisees convicted them that their past actions showed no more value than what they were condemning in the woman taken in adultery. Therefore, they had no right to cast the first stone (see John 8:7–9).

> So when they continued asking Him, He raised Himself up and said to them, "He who is without sin among you, let him throw a stone at her first." And again He stooped down and wrote on the ground. Then those who heard it, being convicted by their conscience, went out one by one, beginning with the oldest even to the last. And Jesus was left alone, and the woman standing in the midst.

Paul shows that the conscience of a person is capable of judging any attempt on his part to deceive. The apostle wrote, "I tell the truth in Christ, I am not lying, my conscience also bearing me witness in the Holy Spirit" (Rom. 9:1).

---

[12] George Eldon Ladd, *A Theology of the New Testament*, (Grand Rapids" Wm. B. Eerdmans Publishing Co, 1993), 519.

Paul also shows that the conscience has the ability to judge one's walk with God relative to being crafty and another's handling of the Word of God to be deceitful. Paul the apostle teaches, "But we have renounced the hidden things of shame, not walking in craftiness nor handling the word of God deceitfully, but by manifestation of the truth commending ourselves to every man's conscience in the sight of God" (2 Cor. 4:2).

The consciences of people could judge the value of Paul's actions, including his handling of the Word of God, relative to how they manifested the truth of God.

Another important matter about the conscience is that it apparently can be programmed or educated. The following passages show the conscience that has been conditioned against godly values:

> ...speaking lies in hypocrisy, having their own conscience seared with a hot iron" (1 Tim. 4:2).
>
> To the pure all things are pure, but to those who are defiled and unbelieving nothing is pure; but even their mind and conscience are defiled. They profess to know God, but in works they deny Him, being abominable, disobedient, and disqualified for every good work (Titus 1:15–16).

That the conscience can be programmed negatively against God suggests that it can also be conditioned or programmed for godliness. For the sake of orderly thinking, let us assume that the evidence is conclusive that the conscience can indeed be programmed or educated in regard to its capacity to make value-judgments. Accordingly, we understand that if the conscience has been properly programmed, it judges great value only in what builds God's kingdom. John Wesley's comprehensive overview of the conscience provides a hypothesis for this view:

> Conscience, then, is that faculty whereby we are at once conscious of our own thoughts, words and actions; of their merit or demerit, of their being good or bad; and, consequently, deserving either praise or censure. Some pleasure generally attends the former sentence; some uneasiness the latter. But this varies exceedingly, according to education and a thousand other circumstances.[13]

The conscience can be informed or programmed to respond in uneasiness or pleasure. It can bring to the consciousness our own thoughts, words, and actions of merit or demerit, or their being good or bad. Thoughts are subjective, but words or actions are objective. The terms "pleasure" and "uneasiness" indicate that the conscience tends to express itself in the emotions. This connects instinctive value-judgment to the emotions.

Also, this view of the conscience relates to what modern psychology refers to as the subconscious. Nathaniel Branden suggests that the subconscious is capable of "valuejudgments" and then teaches that an emotion is a "valueresponse" to "value-judgment." [14] He seems to be ascribing to the subconscious what we are thinking only in terms of spiritual value. Apparently the conscience does involve some subconscious mental processes.

---

[13] Wesley, *Wesley's Works,* vol. 75 (Albany, Oregon: Sage Digital Library).

[14] Brandon, *The Psychology of Self-Esteem* (New York: Bantam Books), 68, 69.

But by looking at the subconscious aspects of the conscience in its biblical context, we get a more God-influenced view of its function in the personality than in modern psychology.

Also, we are not suggesting that the conscience is limited to subconscious awareness. We are only suggesting that its function is primarily intuitive. The more rational understanding that supports this intuitiveness takes place in the intellect as a function of the mind.

Taking notice of the faculties of the heart and their capacities makes it possible to identify the root causes of their dysfunction. This gives us a foundation for understanding how
God wants to restore the heart to spiritual productivity.

The Causes for the Heart Soil Being Unproductive

Scripture teaches that there is hardness to the wayside heart. The wayside soil illustrates the perverted heart's lack of understanding that comes from being spiritually "hard of hearing" (Matt. 13:15). This soil was a trodden path along the side of a field. It is far from being tender enough to be open to the grain, much less growing it, just as a hardheaded, hardhearted, closed-minded person is not open to receiving the gospel, "the word of the kingdom." Jesus had other words to say about hardness of heart.

Our Lord associated hardness of heart with unbelief. He rebuked the disciples for their "unbelief and hardness of heart" (Mark 16:14). Evidently the two coexist and each contributes to the other. The development of these characteristics is caused by pride.

Pride often causes a person to have a hardheaded, closed mind. Pharaoh and his people are the most outstanding biblical examples of hearts being hardened. Again and again they agreed to God's terms, only to harden their hearts against God. Nehemiah pointed to the root cause of this hardness when he said, "they acted proudly" (Neh. 9:10). Their prideful hardness was so obstinate that even the miraculous plagues did not teach them enough to save them from destruction in the Red Sea.

Another example is the king, Nebuchadnezzar. His spirit was "hardened in pride" (Dan. 5:20), meaning his pride was responsible for his spirit being hard. This hardness kept him from believing God and taking seriously God's warning from Daniel. As a result, he didn't correct his ways and lost his throne for a time, as God had said he would.

Thayer's Greek Lexicon associates pride with unbelief. It explains that pride is 1) empty braggart talk; 2) an insolent and empty assurance, which trusts in its own power and resources and shamefully despises and violates divine laws and human rights; and 3) an impious and empty presumption which trusts in the stability of earthly things. [15] This prideful unbelief causes deficient spiritual understanding.

Jesus attributed the disciples' lack of understanding to the fact that their "hearts were hardened."

"Then He went up into the boat to them, and the wind ceased. And they were greatly amazed in themselves beyond

---

[15] *Thayer's Greek Lexicon*, Online Bible (Bronson, Michigan: Online Bible USA, 1995).

The Capacities of the Heart

measure, and marveled. For they had not understood about the loaves, because their heart was hardened" (Mark 6:51–52).

Jesus asked them, "Why do you reason because you have no bread? Do you not yet perceive nor understand? Is your heart still hardened?" (Mark 8:17). Since pride causes hardness of heart and unbelief, and hardness and unbelief

---

cause deficient spiritual understanding, it follows that pride is the root cause of deficient spiritual understanding.

This pride, which results in unbelief and deficient spiritual understanding, is a condition of life called the pride of life (see 1 John 2:16). This perversion is a tendency toward Godrejecting self-sufficiency, believing in one's own way as opposed to having faith in God and His way. The result is that the intellect is diverted from understanding salvation's gospel and God's way is rejected.

In the Bible, pride and faith are seen in contrast to each other. Ps. 31:23 states, "Oh, love the LORD, all you His saints! For the LORD preserves the faithful, And fully repays the proud person."

Proverbs 28:25 tells us, "He who is of a proud heart stirs up strife, But he who trusts in the LORD will be prospered." Habakkuk 2:4 states, "Behold the proud, His soul is not upright in him; But the just shall live by his faith." And James 4:6 tells us, "Therefore He says: 'God resists the proud, But gives grace to the humble.'"

The pride of life is a system of impulses that arises from inordinate faith in self, or in humanity in general. It causes the intellect to be conceited, self-sufficient, and spiritually closeminded, resulting in false understanding. This hardened condition that refuses to depend on God, and thus counteracts faith, is depicted in the wayside soil.

The Cause of the Stony Heart

The stony soil of Palestine consists of a hard rock pan topped with good soil. This kind of condition was present in the parable. The rock pan blocked the roots of the newly germinated seeds from reaching into the deeper nutritious soil for the purpose of growing plants that would produce fruit. The stone depicts resistance to spiritual growth. Stoniness also served as a metaphor of resistance to God in the Old Testament.

> I will give them one heart, and I will put a new spirit within them, and take the stony heart out of their flesh, and give them a heart of flesh, that they may walk in My statutes and keep My judgments and do them; and they shall be my people, and I will be their God (Ezek. 11:19–20).
>
> I will give you a new heart and put a new spirit within you; I will take the heart of stone out of your flesh and give you a heart of flesh. I will put My Spirit within you and cause you to walk in My statutes, and you will keep My judgments and do them (Ezek. 36:26–27).

The "heart of stone" in this Scripture is consistent with the picture of the parable. Both the "heart of stone" and the "stony soil" depict resistance to God. This stony resistance is a selfish kind of love with a sensory orientation. This is the lust of the flesh (see 1 John 2:16). The Wesley Bible defines the lust of the flesh as "sin-tainted human desires." [16] These desires constitute unholy love and cause stony resistance to the love

---

[16] *Wesley Bible*, 1 John 2:16 notes, p.1893

of God, which is love for God as well as love for truth and people.

The Bible shows these loves opposing each other:
> For the flesh lusts against the Spirit and the Spirit against the flesh; and these are contrary to one another, so that you do not do the things that you wish. But if you are led by the Spirit, you are not under the law. Now the works of the flesh are evident, which are: adultery, fornication, uncleanness, lewdness, idolatry, sorcery, hatred, contentions, jealousies, outbursts of wrath, selfish ambitions, dissensions, heresies, envy, murders, drunkenness, revelries, and the like; of which I tell you beforehand, just as I also told you in time past, that those who practice such things will not inherit the kingdom of God (Gal. 5:17–21).

The flesh, in this context, is the human nature operating apart from God. It is original depravity acquiring more and more depravity. The lust of the flesh is a system of impulses that arises from preoccupation with sensory experience. This causes the will to resist God and the salvation He gives. This selfish, self-centered, resisting condition that counteracts the love of God is depicted in the stony soil.

The Cause of the Thorny Heart

The thorny soil allowed the seeds to germinate and put forth plants, showing that new spiritual life was born, but the nutrients of the soil were all absorbed by the roots of the thorns. When the conscience places more value in the material and the earthly than in godliness and eternal things, an emotional, inordinate fascination develops for material things. This precludes an enthusiasm for Jesus, as thorns preclude the normal growth of good plants. Consequently, people are left to the continued unspiritual and worldly influence that causes them to hope in material things. This is the lust of the eyes (1 John 2:16). The Wesley Bible defines the "lust of the eyes" as "Greed for more and more things."[17]

The Bible contrasts earthly, materialistic hope with hope in God. Proverbs 10:28 states, "The hope of the righteous will

---

be gladness, But the expectation of the wicked will perish." Proverbs 11:7 tells us, "When a wicked man dies, his expectation will perish. And the hope of the unjust perishes." Psalm 62:10 reads, "Do not trust in oppression, Nor vainly hope in robbery; If riches increase, Do not set your heart on them." In Job 11:20 we read, "But the eyes of the wicked will fail, And they shall not escape, And their hope—loss of life!" Psalm 33:17 explains, "A horse is a vain hope for safety; Neither shall it deliver any by its great strength." In Psalm 31:24 we read, "Be of good courage, And He shall strengthen your heart, All you who hope in the LORD." Psalm 146:5 explains, "Happy is he who has the God of Jacob for his help, Whose hope is in the LORD his God." In Jeremiah 29:11, we see "'For I know the thoughts that I think toward you,' says the LORD, 'thoughts of peace and not of evil, to give you a future and a hope.'" Lamentations 3:24 tells us, "'The LORD is my portion,' says my soul, 'Therefore I hope in Him!'"

The lust of the eyes is a system of impulses that arises from the conscience's inordinate fascination with material things. This greedy condition of false hope that chokes true hope is depicted in the thorny soil.

---

[17] Wesley Bible, 1 John 2:16 notes, p.1893.

God's Original Design Perverted

God designed people to function by the dominant influence of the Spirit by being filled with the Spirit. Adam and Eve had been functioning this way from their beginning. When they moved away from the Spirit's influence, beginning with Eve moving toward the forbidden fruit, their drives, passions, and impulses, that were good in themselves, became misdirected. Then when they acted on this perversion, the break with God became fully realized.

They lost for all humankind the privilege of being born into this world in right relationship with God. Having lost this relationship, people became self-centered instead of Godcentered. The natural tendency toward faith in God was turned into inordinate faith in oneself—the pride of life. The natural tendency to love God with all the heart, soul, and mind (Matt. 22:37) was turned into inordinate self-love, self-centeredness focusing on the sensory—the lust of the flesh (1 John 2:16). Hope, rooted in the hope of eternal life (Titus 3:7), was turned into hope in "this present world" (2 Tim. 4:10)—the lust of the eyes.

The Edenic tree represented the fruit of self-centeredness as an alternative to the fruit of the Spirit (see Galatians 5:22). A study can be made of these three evil avenues to the soul in the temptation of Eve and the temptations of Christ. All three are clearly present.

First, Eve saw that the tree was good for food. As she began to give way to her cravings, they soon became stronger than her love for God and truth. This broke the determination of her will to hold to what God had said was good. Formerly, she had loved what God loved too much for physical appetite to overcome her regard for Him. But now physical appetite began to strongly influence her judgment of what was good or evil. Her will remained strong through the love of God. But with her move toward evil, her will became dominated by the sensory, taking on a sensualistic twist. God had wanted her will to be acting through the love of God, "love as a choice"[18]

---

based on "esteem and approbation"[20] for Him—not driven by appetite. The will was to be dominant over such distractions—not dominated by animalistic drives. This development was the lust of the flesh and this caused the loss of the dominion of love.

Second, Eve saw that the tree was pleasant to the eyes. This fascination with the natural beauty became hope in the material. What appealed to the eye became a primary factor in her judgment of what was good or evil. This choked out the voice of conscience that had been content to place hope in God. As a result, her conscience's instinctive judgment of what was right and good for her became warped by a false materialistic sense of value. Thus the conscience that had been focused on the value of the spiritual and the eternal became dominated by a fascination with the material to the point it took on a materialistic twist. This development was the lust of the eyes, the loss of the dominion of hope.

Third, Eve saw that the tree was a tree desirable to make one wise. Her ego began to demand self-gained, prideful knowledge with the fanciful wish to be equal with or "like God" (see Genesis 3:5). And this became an overwhelming factor in her consideration of where she should place her faith and of what was good or evil. She was ready to place faith in

---

[18] *The Zondervan Pictorial Encyclopedia of the Bible* (Grand Rapids: Zondervan Publishing House, 1980), 1990, 1st col.

knowledge that could be gained apart from God. This leaning to her own understanding (see Proverbs 3:5) seemed to be a more self-gratifying and prestigious way than "the way of truth" (see 2 Peter 2:2) that could be gained only by faith.

---

[20] Kenneth Wuest, *Word Studies in the Greek New Testament,* vol. 3 (Grand Rapids: Wm. B. Eerdmans Publishing Company, 1983), 60–62.

Thus the intellect's former perception and understanding that had been dominated by faith became blinded from truth by an inordinate, self-reliant quest for knowledge dominated by pride. This development was the pride of life, the loss of the dominion of faith. Eve's faith had been essentially a perception of God's importance to her life, as opposed to pride's idea of self-importance, making her God-reliant instead of self-reliant. Thayer says, "Pride is an insolent and empty assurance which trusts in its own power and resources and shamefully despises and violates divine laws."[19]

The will chose in terms of physical appetite. The conscience judged value in terms of what fascinated the eyes. And the intellect understood in terms of prideful, worldly knowledge. Thus these very faculties that God had given to people to center them on Himself became perverted to center on the self, or ego, of those people.

By this analysis we see that God did not create people with lustful inclinations to sin, but by the misapplication of Godgiven drives, passions, and impulses; lust after sin developed. Neither did God insert depravity in the heart as a curse after the first couple sinned. Rather, the loss of

---

[19] *Thayer's Greek Lexicon*, Online Bible, (Bronson, Michigan: Online Bible U.S.A., 1995).

relationship with God that had been maintained by the God-centrality of faith, love, and hope now caused people to center their drives, passions, and impulses on ego. This self-centeredness became the essence of the depravity that came to them.

Jesus showed the way to victory over depravity when He was tempted through the same three avenues to the soul as Eve was. First, He was tempted to turn bread into stone against God's will, a temptation of the lust of the flesh. Second, He

---

was tempted to follow Satan's strategy to conquer the world, a temptation of the lust of the eyes. Third, He was tempted to show off by throwing Himself down from the pinnacle of the temple, a temptation of the pride of life.

Jesus conquered these temptations through God's Word instead of doubting God's Word as Eve did. He chose against the wrong gratification of physical appetite because He loved God and did not "live by bread alone" (Luke 4:4). He judged against Satan's strategy to conquer the world because He placed His hope in God Who said, "You shall worship the LORD your God and Him only you shall serve" (Luke 4:8). Because God's Word said, "You shall not tempt the LORD your God" (Luke 4:12), He understood that He couldn't have faith in God to protect Him if He were to throw Himself down from the pinnacle of the temple.

Expressions of Evil

None of the three systems of evil operate separately. All are expressed in the lust of the flesh. For example, the pride of life often expresses itself in hatred, contentions, outbursts of wrath, jealousies, envy, etc. These are listed as "works of the flesh" (see Galatians 5:19–21) which result from the lusting of the flesh (see Galatians 5:17). The lust of the eyes also expresses itself in works of the flesh: adultery, fornication, lewdness, idolatry, murders, drunkenness, etc. Therefore, both the pride of life and the lust of the eyes are expressed in the lust of the flesh.

The sin process begins with inordinate, sensual self-love. This leads to pride and inordinate fascination with the human body along with the rest of the material world, which in turn causes worshiping and serving the creature rather than the Creator (see Romans 1:25). The end result is lust for inordinately possessing and experiencing other human bodies and obsession with other material things, which is a perverted love. Of course, this lust for the outer self and the material precludes spiritual development and bars people from Godinfluence and God-dominance.

Reinhold Niebuhr gives further insight to this. He said,
> If we discount Hellenistic theology with its inclination to make sensuality the primary sin and to derive it from the natural inclinations of the physical life, we must arrive at the conclusion that Christian theology, in both its Augustinian and semi-Augustinian (Thomistic) forms, regards sensuality (even in general) as a derivative of the more primal sin of self-love. Sensuality represents a further confusion consequent upon the original confusion of substituting the self for God as the centre of existence. Man, having lost the true centre of his life, is no longer able to maintain his own will as the centre of himself. [20]

Of particular interest is Niebuhr's recognition of sensualism being rooted in self-love (or self-centeredness) and the influence of both on the will.

---

[20] Reinhold Niebuhr, *Nature and Destiny of Man,* vol. 1 (London: Nisbet and Co., 1946), 247.

Contemporary terms show the three systems of evil. The pride of life is humanism. The lust of the flesh is sensualism. And the lust of the eyes is materialism. Webster supports this, showing that humanism is any system or mode of thought or action in which human interests, values, and dignity predominate, especially an ethical theory that often rejects the importance of a belief in God.

The "sensual" is defined as arousing or being preoccupied with the gratification of the senses or appetites. "Carnal" is defined as lacking in moral restraints. "Sensualism" is a dedication or subjection to sensual appetites. And "materialism" is the preoccupation with or emphasis on material objects, comforts, and considerations, as opposed to spiritual or intellectual values. [21] The lust of the fleshsensualism drives the will with pride of life-humanism, and lust of the eyes-materialism. This causes the will to choose to act in various evil ways.

The basic problem with the depraved heart can be discovered in how it responds to three questions: "Where should I focus my capacity for faith?" "Where should I focus my capacity for love?" "Where should I focus my capacity for hope?" The depraved heart says, "I place my faith in my own wisdom (humanism)." It says, "I am preoccupied with loving what pleasures my senses and makes me feel good (sensualism)." Thus I am characterize as those who are "lovers of pleasure rather than lovers of God" (2 Tim 3:4). And the depraved heart states, "I place my hope in earthly,

---

[21] The Random House Webster's Electronic Dictionary & Thesaurus, college edition (WordPerfect Corporation, 1994)

material things (materialism)." This was how Eve and Adam answered, and this self-centered response depraved the heart. Why? Because the heart cannot properly function on self-centeredness for it is designed to be plugged-in to God and to be interfaced with God-centeredness. Only with this dynamic connection, can it properly function.

———————

Plugged-in to the Dynamic Word

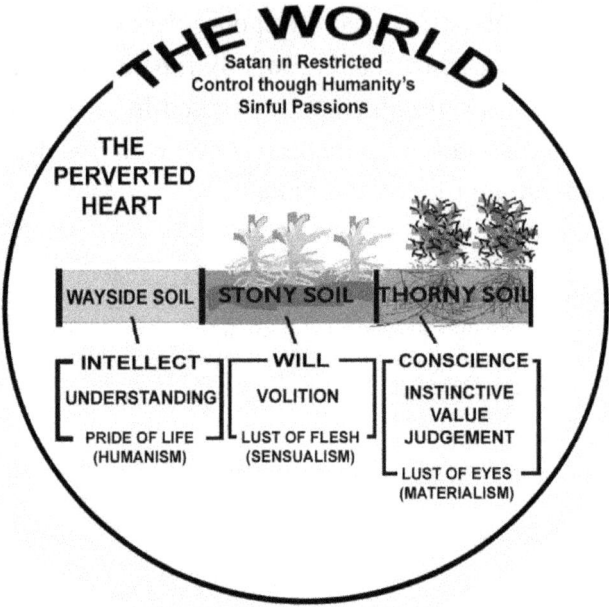

CHAPTER 4 The Nature of Truth

In order to fulfill its mission a ship must reckon with truth. It must adjust its rudder and sails to the water current that exists and the winds that prevail. In short, the ship must reckon with reality. Usually we think of truth as a true report of reality. But a report is only true to the extent it accurately defines what exists. The reality is what truly exists. Therefore truth can be thought of as the reality itself.

Where the Bible uses the word, truth, it often refers to reality. For example, where Jesus says, "the truth shall make you free" (John 8:32), Jesus is pointing to the reality that truth will, by its very existing presence in our lives, liberate us from the bondage of falsehood. More specifically, with this statement, Jesus is referring to the truth-reality of His salvation—what God has put into existence to free us from our sin. In this context, we need to reckon with the reality of our sin-need and what Christ offers for that need. However, if we further investigate the nature of truth we have both a greater understanding of the salvation it offers and a better understanding of the Bible, because truth is the foundation of the Word.

We have established that God works through faith, love, and hope, and that these dynamics work in the heart. We list faith, love, and hope in this order because that is the order in which they usually correlate with other triads expressing these dynamics, as we shall see. In this chapter we will observe how God's truth-program is put into play by Jesus and how Jesus,

Himself, in the process, functions through faith, love, and hope. These observations will reveal how the triad is integrated with the character of Jesus and the truth with which He identifies Himself, when He says, "I am the way, the truth, and the life" (John 14:6).

Pilate asked Jesus, "Are you a king?" Jesus answered, "You say rightly that I am a king. For this cause I was born, and for this cause I have come into the world, that I should bear witness to the truth. Everyone who is of the truth hears My voice" (John 18:37).

King Jesus declared that His mission was to bear witness to the truth. His kingship was dedicated to the conquest of falsehood by exposing the world to truth. To do this, He was willing to go to the cross, knowing that if He would be lifted up (see John 12:32) He would draw all people to Himself. In doing so, He would draw them to the truth.

When Jesus stood before Pilate to be judged, Pilate failed to recognize the truth because he was not committed to "obeying the truth" (Rom. 2:8). How different was King David's attitude—the king who was a very important figure in the lineage of King Jesus. He prayed, "Show me Your ways, O LORD; Teach me Your paths. Lead me in Your truth and teach me, For You are the God of my salvation; On You I wait all the day (Ps. 25:4–5).

As we seek God and wait on Him instead of leaning on our "own understanding" (see Proverbs 3:5), the "truth" will be revealed to us. Jesus said, "If you abide in My word, you are My disciples indeed. And you shall know the truth, and the truth shall make you free" (John 8:31–32). This abiding in the word involves abiding both in biblical knowledge and in obedience to the commands of the Bible. Hence, discernment of the "truth" (1 Cor. 2:14) arises from a Spirit-enabled, holistic study of Scripture, motivated by a desire to follow the truth that is to be discovered.

The Importance of Truth

God's will incorporates the truth-reality of life and human design. To live accordingly is to experience life to the fullest. Performing contrary to God's will is a false way because such performance does not recognize the truth of human design nor consider God's dealings with such behavior. Since God has designed our bodies and personalities, He knows for what purpose we were designed and how we should function. Therefore, to deliberately go against God's will is gross blindness to truth and the height of foolishness. This is sin, for sin is lawlessness in regard to God's law (see 1 John 3:4). Sin makes people dysfunctional.

If one tries to operate a machine such as a car without changing the oil and using proper fuel, and then drives it on terrain it was not designed for, the car will soon break down. The designer of the auto knows more about the machine than anyone else. Therefore, his instructions should be obeyed. For someone to take the attitude that the designer and manufacturer of the car has no business telling the driver of the car how it should be operated is the height of foolishness.

Nevertheless, this is the attitude that many people seem to have toward God about themselves. Others have tried to convince themselves that the designer-creator-God did not mean what He said, and/or they have tried to rationalize around His instructions in one way or another. Such irresponsibility is a false way. It should be obvious that the truth that our designer-creator-God reveals to us in His Bibleoperators-manual is the only path to functionality and spiritual conquest.

But what is truth? We have shown that the Bible often refers to reality when it uses the word, truth. First and foremost, truth is existential reality. "Truth is what I become before God as I am transformed into the image of Christ and experience the realities of what the Lord Jesus has accomplished. What is reality? Truth is reality, Jesus is the truth (John 14:6); this should be our reality."[22]

Yes, truth is more than just a true report; it is also reality. To begin, we need to consider that Jesus is the truth (as well as the way and the life) as recorded in John 14:6. And the fact that Jesus is the truth incorporates the reality that He is also the way and the life. "The way" is a phase of truth; it is the truth in the sense that it reveals what Jesus has done to save us and in the sense that it shows how to how we can appropriate that salvation Jesus provided. This means that the way is truthrevealed. "The life" is another phase of truth; it is the operation of truth in a person that produces a Christian life for that individual. This means that the life is truth-operative. Thus the way and the life are embodied in the truth and constitute two other phases of truth.

To illustrate the three phases of truth and how they relate to each other, think about chairs. It is a simple fact that chairs exist. They are not figments of our imagination or things that exist only in our dreams. Chairs do exist in real life. This is *the truth*—truth-reality. But suppose certain people didn't know that chairs existed or how to use them?

---

[22] Watchman Nee, compiled by Sentinel Kulp, (New Kensington, PA: Whitaker House, 1998).

The truth of the chairs would need to be revealed to them by tongue or pen. However,

---

this revelation is also inherit in the chair itself. By observing the design of the chair, the uninformed could discover the truth-revealed in the chair by which he would know the chair's use with out anyone explaining it to him. Thus, the truthreality of the chair incorporates the truth-revealed in the chair. Likewise, the truth-reality (the truth) of Jesus incorporates the truth-revealed (the way) in Jesus.

However, revelation is not enough. People must seat themselves in the available chairs and remain there to rest. In so doing, they act upon the light they have received, knowing that this act will appropriate the benefits of the chairs. As they rest in the chairs, they experience the truth-operative that provides a life of support and comfort. This shows that truthreality of the chair also incorporates the truth-operative in the use of the chair. Likewise, the truth-reality (the truth) of Jesus incorporates the truth-operative (the life) in experiencing Jesus.

Jesus is all three phases of truth. He is *the truth* as truthreality for he is our salvation (see 2 Timothy 2:10; Psalm 25:5). He is truth-revealed, for He shows us "the way of truth" that Peter mentions in 2 Peter 2:2—*the way* of resting in the salvation-chair by asking us to abide in Him (see John 15:4). He is truth-operative, "for in Him we live and move and have our being" (Acts 17:28) and thus experience *the life* of resting in the salvation-chair. Of course, this life of resting-in-Jesus support is also actively serving Him.

Three Phases of Truth Relative to Faith, Love, and Hope

We need to receive the truth in all of its phases in order receive its benefits. We could say that we need to be interfaced with the way, the truth, and the life. Interface is a computer term so those who don't know a lot about computers may not understand. Therefore let me explain: A letter can be typed into a computer and seen on its monitor screen. But for the letter to be printed out on paper so that it can be sent to its intended recipient, the characteristics of the computer need to be plugged-in to a printer. We call this interfacing; the computer is interfaced with the printer by a cord so the printer can receive the computer's characteristics.

God has means for us to be interfaced with the characteristics of truth (the three phases of truth that we have discussed) so that we can receive the benefits of truth. These means are faith, love, and hope.

Faith Interfaces Us with the Way

Faith is the intellect's spiritual understanding, or comprehension. As faith comprehends the truth, it believes it (see 2 Thessalonians 2:13), but it believes as a result of encounter with the way—the revelation that we must trust Jesus as our Savior and follow Him. Then, as belief matures into trust, it signals the will to demonstrate trust by purposefully trusting Jesus for salvation. Ultimately, faith is the way, because we are "saved through faith" (see Ephesians 2:8). Faith is the way of appropriating God's truth to our lives—the way of receiving Jesus as our Savior—and the way of doing God's will in our walk with the Lord. "We walk by faith" (2 Cor. 5:7). This is why James said, "I will show you my faith by my works" (James 2:18).

Also, as we follow God's way, we are bound to observe from experience that this way to God is also the way to a fulfilled, highly functional life. This gives us more belief and trust in the way.

Therefore, *faith* is a dynamic element that directly interfaces us with *the way*.

Love Interfaces Us with the Truth

Love is inseparably connected to the truth. God's love for truth demanded that He keep his promise to punish sin, but His love for humanity clung to the truth that people needed a savior. Consequently, we have love's ultimate act, the truth that "Christ died for the ungodly" (Rom. 5:6). This provision of truth for truth is God's ultimate demonstration of love's identity with truth.

As people respond to this love-act in repentance and faith, they receive love, the love of God which causes them to love what God loves and hate what He hates. Basically, love loves the truth and hates falsehood. And, love gives the will the power to choose to obey the truth because it is centered on doing God's will rather than being like "those who are selfseeking and do not obey the truth" (Rom. 2:8). Yes, love is inseparably connected to the truth.

Christians love the way and the life. But this should perpetuate an even greater romance with the truth because truth is basic to the way and the life. If the greatest love is for the way, legalism may be the result. If the greatest love is for the life, too much emphasis on the benefits of Christianity and not enough on commitment may result. Therefore, genuine love, the greatest of faith, love, and hope, is focused on truth, the greatest of the way, the truth, and the life. And basic truth says that "God is love" (see 1 John 4:16). Therefore, *love* is a dynamic element that directly interfaces us with *the truth* through which we also loves the way and the life.

Hope Interfaces Us with the Life

The life is hope being fulfilled. Hope develops the Christian life, but when hope is low spiritual enthusiasm is low. This translates into lack of fervent praying, lackluster worship services, and little desire to witness to Christ. When Christians have a lot of hope, it inspires them to fervently go all out for God and enthusiastically engage in the battle for truth. Hope also inspires Christians to lead others to the fountain of life. Thus it continually perpetuates the life. In short, hope is the breath in the life's lungs—the life that is eternal life.

The more one truly lives in Christ the more he sees Jesus as the hope of life. Jesus said, "I have come that they may have life, and that they may have it more abundantly" (John 10:10). Therefore, *hope* is a dynamic element that directly interfaces us with *the life*. Faith, love, and hope are imparted to us as a part of God's truth program.

By the way, our illustration of printing a letter from a computer relates to what the Bible says about us Christians in 2 Cor. 3:2, "You are our epistle written in our hearts, known and read by all men." As we become interfaced with Jesus and His truth, our lives become epistles (letters) which people can read to see Jesus' characteristics, His beauty. This will attract some of them to Jesus.

The Interaction of Faith, Love, and Hope Relative to the Way, the Truth and the Life

Just as the way and the life are incorporated in the truth, faith and hope are incorporated in love. This is why love "believes all things, hopes all things" (1 Cor. 13:7). The truth is expressed through the way and the life as love is expressed through faith and hope. Also, just as love is the greatest of its triad, so truth is the greatest of its triad. The other members of love's triad are nothing without love. And the other members of the truth's triad are nothing without truth.

The lust of the eyes-humanism is perverted faith, the lust of the flesh-sensualism is perverted love, and the lust of the eyes-materialism is perverted hope. As such they form a triad structure of falsehood. Humanism and materialism are incorporated in sensualism. Sensualism's way is humanism and its life is materialism (the objects it lusts for are material or earthly, including the out-side-of-marriage bodies it lusts to experience sexually. Therefore, this triad is targeted to be destroyed by the truth triad.

Humanism, sensualism, and materialism are in direct opposition to faith, love, and hope respectively. These systems of evil are set in array against the dynamics of truth. So the battle lines are drawn as faith, love, and hope go on the offensive against them for spiritual conquest. The battle is the Lord's (see 1 Samuel 17:47; 2 Chronicles 20:15), but the victory is wrought though people.

Since faith, love, and hope are a part of the truth-program embodied in Jesus. Jesus is about faith, love, and hope as well as the way, the truth, and the life. And Jesus came to conquer falsehood by exposing it to the truth that He embodies. As truth in its three phases, Jesus can dismantle the very structure of falsehood—the very structure of its perverted reality, its false revelation of reality, and its resultant dysfunctional operation.

The Logos and His Identification with the Three Phases of Truth

The "Logos" of John 1:1 is a concept that lends evidence to Jesus being three phases of truth. The word "Logos," as John applies the word from its etymological roots in Greek and Jewish culture, is Jesus in the capacity of His divine creative, illuminating, controlling, sustaining mind, according to William Barclay.[23]

As such, we could view Jesus as truth-reality (sustaining mind), truth-revealed (illuminating mind), and truth-operative (controlling mind). The grace in Him activates and applies this creative, controlling, revealing truth in people's lives. And this divine vitality is intended to give Christians vibrant productivity, self-control, and power to make a dynamic spiritual difference in the world. However, this happens in direct ratio to the degree of surrender and dedication to Jesus, because only as one surrenders to Jesus can Jesus live in that one and exert His influence.

Gordon Clark tells us something else about the Logos. He indicates that the "English cognate" of the Logos in John 1:1 in the Greek is "Logic—the science of valid reasoning"—rather than "Word." In connection with this he says, "If one hesitates to translate the verse as, 'In the beginning was divine Logic,' at least one can say, 'in the beginning was Wisdom.' This translation is accurate enough; it preserves the connotations: and it conveys a satisfactory meaning to the average mind."[24]

Therefore, Jesus, who is the creative, sustaining, controlling, revealing influence, is also the wisdom or logic of this influence. We could think of Him as the physics of the

---

creative, illuminating, controlling, sustaining influence. Physics is the science of matter and energy and their

---

[23] William Barclay, *The Gospel of John*, (Louisville, London: Westminster John Knox Press, 2001), 40–43.
[24] Gordon H. Clark, *The Johannine Logos* (Jefferson, Maryland: The Trinity Foundation, 1972), 19.

interaction. In the capacity of wisdom, Jesus is "upholding all things by the word of His power" (see Hebrews 1:3). Thus we could think of Him as the physics of all material matter and energy and their interaction. But more importantly, in this way of thinking, He is also the physics of all spiritual reality and energy and their interaction—the dynamic logic of the spiritual motion that results in spiritual productivity.

As the Logos, Jesus is identified with all three phases of truth. And, as such, He can dismantle Satan's false revelation of reality and its dysfunctional operation in individuals and society.

Not only is Jesus identified with the Logos and all that it implies, Jesus is identified with God's spoken word. How do we know this? Jesus Himself said, in praying to the Father, "Your word is truth" (John 17:17), obviously referring to God's spoken word. Therefore, because Jesus is the truth and God's word is truth, then it follows that Jesus is identified with God's spoken word recorded in the Bible. He enters the life of people through this spoken/written word as people open their hearts to it. And furthermore, when we compare the characteristics of this word of God with the characteristics of the Logos we find a clear correlation. Jesus is clearly identified with each. We know God's word spoke the worlds into existence; that is creative influence. Very obviously, that is an illuminating influence. And God's word is "upholding all things by the word of His power" (Heb. 1:3); that is, controlling, sustaining influence. As John Paterson, in *The Goodly Fellowship of the Prophets,* has put it, according to William Barclay, "The spoken word to the Hebrews was fearfully alive... It was a unit of energy charged with power. It flies like a bullet to its billet."[25]

This creative, illuminating, controlling, sustaining Jesus, who is the very embodiment of truth, wants to enter and occupy the lives and personalities of His people. And only as He does this can He build a structure of truth-reality in people that will eventually dismantle the perverted reality of falsehood. Jesus enters and occupies lives and personalities through the word that comes to people as they hear it and obey it. This is what is depicted in the sowing of the seed-word in the heart soil described in the parable of the sower.

Through hearing and obeying God's word, people eat of Jesus, for His "flesh is food indeed," and His "blood is drink indeed" (see John 6:55). Thus Christians experience Jesus initially by receiving the word and subsequently by following His teachings and obeying His commands.

Grace Applying Truth

Jesus is "full of grace and truth" (John 1:14) and "grace and truth have come through Jesus" (John 1:17). Therefore, as Jesus comes to the Christians through the word, grace and truth come to them. This grace applies the truth, for Paul says, "For by grace you have been saved through faith, and that not of yourselves; it is the gift of God," (Eph. 2:8). The active agent (the catalyst) of the word-truth is the grace.

The Bible is God's Word, His truth-revelation to people. As people read it and become plugged-in to the Bible's story of spiritual conquest in terms of faith, love, and hope, their hearts acquire a spiritual orientation. To use a modern term,

---

[25] William Barclay, *The Gospel of John* (Louisville, London: Westminster John Knox Press, 2001).

their hearts become interfaced with Scripture. This causes people to follow God's way. Isaiah speaks prophetically, in metaphorical terms, of God's way as the "Highway of Holiness." The prophet said, "The unclean shall not pass over it, But it shall be for others. Whoever walks the road, although a fool, Shall not go astray" (Isaiah 35:8).

To illustrate the motion of God's truth-program of faith, love, and hope operating in hearts that are plugged-in to the Bible, we can visualize a motorized vehicle traveling Isaiah's Highway of Holiness. Our hearts are the wheels of God's kingdom-vehicle that propel it on the Highway of Holiness. The Bible, being the Word of God, is the hub of the heartwheels and their faith-love-hope tires. The power to rotate the Bible-hubs comes from God's truth-engine, which in turn rotates the heart-wheels with the faith-love-hope-tires. The grace-transmission applies the truth-power to the wheels through Jesus, the drive shaft: "For the law was given through Moses, but grace and truth came through Jesus Christ" (John 1:17).

The steep old-covenant-law mountain is leveled before the approach of this advancing kingdom-vehicle to become the foundation of the new covenant "righteousness of faith" (see Romans 4:13). This righteousness is the substance that paves the Highway of Holiness.

The valleys of despair are also filled. The crooked places of liberalism are straightened. And the rough places of legalism are smoothed (see Isaiah 40:4), so that God's kingdom can readily advance on this highway in conquest of all opposing forces. Satan marshals all of his forces of humanism, sensualism, and materialism in a furious fight, but they are destined to be crushed under the faith-love-hope-tires of the kingdom-vehicle. He cannot stop the advance of God's kingdom.

Truth came through Jesus (see John 1:17), so the conquest of God's truth-program that happens in faith, love, and hope throughout the Bible happens in Jesus. We state that the central motif of the Bible is spiritual conquest through faith, love, and hope, but of course this conquest happens in Jesus. The reason spiritual conquest happens in Jesus through faith, love, and hope is that this triad makes self-centered people God-centered through focusing their attention on Jesus.

Thus self-centeredness, the essence of sin, is overcome, or conquered. To look at the Bible through the lens of this motif, or key idea, which is spiritual conquest through faith, love, and hope, is to unlock the basic truths of the Bible. How? We will see the Bible making sense through this view to its passages. And Scriptures, otherwise obscure, will come to light. Thus our study will confirm that our proposed motif or key idea is indeed the central, reoccurring theme and structural fabric of the Bible.[28][29][26]

---

[28] "Is myself Christ-centred or self-centred? ...Did you ever notice what it was that Satan antagonized in Jesus? God-realization. He wanted to alter the centre. 'Do God's work your own way, you are His Son, work for that centre.' ...To get eccentric, off the centre, is exactly what Satan wants us to do. One thing he makes his business, and that is to dethrone God's rule in the heart. The superiority of Christ's self was that He was God-centred. Is that the superiority of yourself?" Oswald Chambers, *Biblical Psychology* (Cincinnati, Ohio: God's Revivalist Office, 1914), 194–195.

[29] "The flesh makes self the center of all things, while the spirit centers all life on Christ. Such is the battle that rages in all believers until victory is

---

[26] "Egocentricity is identified by classical Christian theology as the essence of sin." Ray Dunning, *Sanctification, A Layman's Guide,* (Kansas City, Missouri: Beacon Hill Press, 1991).

gained over self." Watchman Nee, compiled by Sentinel Kulp (New Kensington, PA: Whitaker House, 1998), 195.

George Eldon Ladd says, "Modern scholarship is quite unanimous in the opinion that the Kingdom of God was the central image of Jesus."[27]

John Bright says, "For the concept of the Kingdom of God involves, in a real sense, the total message of the Bible."[28] Ladd also shows that God's kingdom is "the dynamic reign or kingly rule of God, and derivatively, the sphere in which the rule is experienced."[29] And in connection with this, he also states that "the theology of the kingdom of God is essentially one of conflict and conquest over the kingdom of Satan."[30]

The focus of our motif, relative to this theme, is on the question of how the kingdom of God conquers the kingdom of Satan. This focus shows that Jesus conquers, as King of the kingdom, by bearing witness to the truth, and that grace applies this truth-sword of conquest in the dynamic processes of faith, love, and hope. Therefore, our motif is in keeping with the motif identified by accepted scholarship.

---

[27] Ladd, A *Theology of the New Testament* (Grand Rapids: William Eerdmans Publishing Co, 1993), 54.

[28] John Bright, *The Kingdom of God* (Nashville: Abingdon Press, 1981), 7.

[29] Ladd, *A Theology of the New Testament* (Grand Rapids: William B. Eerdmans Publishing Co, 1993), 109.

[30] Ladd, *A Theology of the New Testament* (Grand Rapids: William B. Eerdmans Publishing Co, 1993), 48.

God's Covenant Relative to This Motif

Walther Eichrodt and others view the covenant as the central motif of the Bible.[31] Certainly God's covenant is an important theme. Its importance lies in the fact that it

---

expresses the terms for receiving and living out the truth. Therefore, the covenant is inseparable from truth and its dynamic processes—and the kingdom of God that truth drives. This too is in keeping with what is accepted by many scholars.

All that has been considered in this chapter point to the three questions proposed in the conclusion of the last chapter: "Where should I focus my capacity for faith?" "Where should I focus my capacity for love?" "And where should I focus my capacity for hope?" These are basic questions that truth resolves with the general answer, "All three should be focused on God." The Holy Spirit wants to plug-in our capacities to God and His truth program so that our hearts can be interfaced with all of truth's benefits.

---

[31] Eichrodt, *Theology of the Old Testament,* vol. 2 (Philadelphia: Westminster Press, 1963).

**Faith, Love, and Hope Added to Agricultural Picture
to Show Process of Conquering the World**

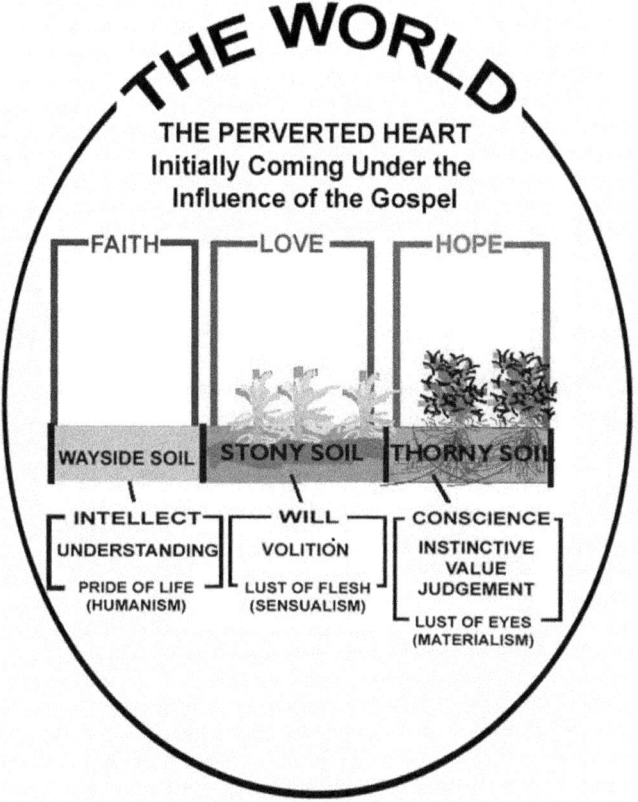

Plugged-in to the Dynamic Word

CHAPTER 5 Faith Restored

For thousands of years it has been understood that a ship needs a captain. When a crisis arises someone must make a decision and give orders. There is no time to call for a meeting of the minds to take a vote. The sailors of the crew understand this and put their full thrust in the captain as they board the ship and subject themselves to his command. Faith is what gives the captain freedom to effectively command the ship and the sailors commitment to their duties. In short, faith provides the proper relationship between captain and crew to have a smooth sailing ship.

The Bible shows us that Captain Jesus is fully trustworthy and asks us to place faith in Him. First, we board the salvationship by faith—and second, we show our faith by obeying the captain's orders and doing our duties aboard the ship. The faith so exercised produces the hope of successfully completing our mission.

As we have seen, early humanity progressively lost all faith-love-hope relationship with God beginning with Adam's and Eve's disobedience. Adam and Eve sinned and broke the covenant they had with God because they lost faith in God. Yet God still kept His part of His covenant even though they did not keep theirs. God did that because the covenant was with humanity in general, not just that first couple, and God cannot lie (see Titus 1:2). For this reason He continued to put His salvation plan into effect. This plan would require people to have the kind of faith that could trust God to be their redeemer by forgiving and removing their sin.

This would be a different faith than that experienced by the first couple in their innocence, for then they did not have sin. Now, after sin entered the picture, people needed the kind of faith that would trust God to provide forgiveness and restoration of man's relationship with God through a Savior.

Depravity in Regard to God's Salvation Plan

The question often arises, "Did God create sin?" The answer is that God created the possibility of sinning by providing freedom of choice, but people, in cooperation with Satan, brought sin into the world. And since the first pair lost the indwelling presence of the Spirit through their sin, all people would be born with the depravity caused by that loss of relationship with God.

Heart depravity, whether it be humanism, sensualism, or materialism, is the natural result of people coming into the world without the indwelling of the Spirit of God. Lack of the Spirit's influence leaves people to the self-centeredness that causes evil. For when natural God-given impulses are centered on God through the dominant influence of the indwelling Spirit, proper faith, love, and hope in God are developed and maintained. But when this influence is lacking, the same impulses become centered on self, causing depravity.

The mind-set that causes this condition is called the "carnal mind" (see Romans 8:7). The Greek for "carnal mind" is *phronema sarkos,* "which indicates a 'mindedness' or 'attitude' toward the flesh—an orientation away from true spirituality and God. It results in a dedication to the body—to animalistic tendencies. This amounts to enmity against

God."[32] The lifestyle lived in this mind-set is what is called "the flesh" that we read about throughout the eighth chapter of Romans.

The carnal mind does not exist independently as a nature, to be distinguished from the human nature. This would give people two natures, as some portray it. Rather, it is the human nature having become depraved. People do not normally possess two natures or personalities. In revising his book, *Conformed to Christ,* Dale Yocum states in the introduction: "Numerous references to 'the sinful nature' have been replaced with other expressions. The former phrase suggests what is not true, that sin is something with an independent 'nature' of its own and that it can exist apart from a moral being. Sin is rather a deformity in human nature, and when it is cleansed, or cured, no entity is removed to be lodged outside. The deformity just ceases to exist in that individual."[37]

The carnal mind-set was the self-centeredness that had come about through God no longer being the center of people's personalities. This was God's basic concern in His plan to restore people to proper relationship with Himself. Not only did this sinful deformity cause people to be self-centered from birth, it caused people to acquire more and more depravity until many people became hopeless victims of their physical drives and emotional passions. Yet even though this inner depravity was God's basic concern, relative to saving

---

[32] Wilber T. Dayton, "The New Testament Conception of Flesh", (Wesleyan Theological Journal, Volume 2 Number 1, Spring 1967).
[37] Yocum, *Conformed to Christ* (Salem, Ohio: Schmul Publishing Co., Inc, 1962), 5–6.

people from sin, people would have to be conditioned for its cure; this would take some time.

The only way this could happen was through the death of a sinless life. A sinless person would have to die in the people's place. One who was guilty of his own sin could not die for the sins of another. Such a person's death would pay only for his own sin. Furthermore, the sinless person would have to be of sufficient quality to atone for all humankind. For even if an ordinary person could have been found who was sinless and willing to die, the offering of his life could have atoned for only one person. Therefore, the offering of a life to die had to be a superior life—a superior person. Only One like God Himself could qualify to die a death that would justly substitute the death that had been promised as a consequence of sin, a death that would be efficacious for all people.

Yet people had to be conditioned to recognize the significance of such a death. In the meantime, a means of forgiving penitent people had to be provided. Therefore, God provided a temporary system of animal sacrifices that pointed to the supreme "offering for sin" (see Isaiah 53:10) that would eventually be offered. The death of the animals sacrificed symbolized the death that sin caused. And the blood involved showed that "without shedding of blood there is no remission" of sin (Heb. 9:22).

However, it needs to be emphasized that "it is not possible that the blood of bulls and goats could take away sins" (Heb. 10:4). By sacrificing animals in obedience to God, people could express penitent faith in God. Therefore, on the basis of their faith, and on the basis of Christ's pending offering, justification was credited to their account. Yet, after they died, they evidently would be in the place of death called Sheol

(Psalm 16:10 gives the Hebrew word for Hades) until Christ would become an "offering for sin" (see Isaiah 53:10).

Evidently the relationship that Adam and Eve had with God after their sin and subsequent reconciliation was relatively distant. The same was true for humanity in general, because the Spirit was no longer dwelling in them to make them spiritually sensitive. Therefore God had to get their attention through natural means. This is why God appeared in human form and spoke in an audible voice and through angels, as we see in the Old Testament.

As time went on, the murder of Abel by Cain and then the murder of a young man by Lamech showed that depravity was on an increase. It was not until the first pair's grandson, Enosh, was born to their younger son, Seth, that God began to get the attention of people to any great degree. "Then men began to call on the name of the LORD" (Gen. 4:26).

A People of Faith

To study the faith of people of the Old Testament, let us review our definitions of faith and hope. Faith is developing belief in God that is formed in the intellect and matures into the choice of the will to trust in God. It is God-reliance as opposed to the kind of self-reliance that diminishes or excludes trust in God.

Hope is faith having laid hold of a specific promise of God. Or, stated another way, it is faith trusting God to fulfill a specific promise that He made. It is also an appraisal of value in God, formed in the conscience, deeming God desirable and trustworthy. The accuracy of these definitions can be determined by how well they fit the usage of these terms in Scripture.

God was mostly revealed as the Father in the Old Testament, and His primary point of contention with people was for their trust in Him. When God had complaints against people it was usually focused on their lack of trust in Him, along with the disobedience that resulted. These complaints were mostly about Israel trusting in idols and the false gods they represented instead of fearing and trusting God. Yet God found some in whom He could develop faith in Himself.

Hebrews 11 is about the faith of some of the most outstanding of these people and how they stood out as striking counterparts to their contemporaries because of their faith. These contemporaries, like the little horn of Daniel's vision, "cast truth to the ground" (see Daniel 8:12) by their disregard for God and His way. On the other hand, the faithful placed their faith in the way of truth and adhered to it, as David articulated. In Psalm 25:4–5, we read, "Show me Your ways, O LORD; Teach me Your paths. Lead me in Your truth and teach me, For You are the God of my salvation; On You I wait all the day."

Remember from our study in the last chapter, faith is a dynamic element that is directly integrated, or interfaced, with the way—the way of truth that God desires for us to take—the way that Jesus says He is. This way can be seen in the "paths" that the faithful Old Testament people took. Jeremiah referred to these paths as "the old paths, where the good way is," and stated that people should "walk in it" to "find rest for your souls," (see Jeremiah 6:16). Faith guides us to, and leads us in, the way that God wants us to take. And by taking this way, we establish a path for others to follow.

In short, Hebrews 11 shows the dividing line that was drawn by faith between the people of God and the people of the world. Outstanding demonstrations of faith were on one side of this line and glaring demonstrations of life apart from faith in God were on the other side. The people of this chapter represent those reconciled to God through His Old Testament program. Therefore, a study of Hebrews 11 will give us a look at the dynamics of the faith that paved the historical paths of the Old Testament way of truth (see Psalm 24:4–5). These paths will further help to show us how faith is woven into the structural fabric of the Bible and turns people to God and away from humanism.

The Faith of Abel

Hebrews 11:4 tells us that "by faith Abel offered to God a more excellent sacrifice than Cain, through which he obtained witness that he was righteous, God testifying of his gifts; and through it he being dead still speaks."

Cain, on the other hand, offered a bloodless sacrifice of vegetables, contrary to the will of God. He was seeking a relationship with God through following the way that was right by his own reasoning. His understanding was clouded by his humanistic leaning on his own understanding (see Proverbs 3:5) instead of placing unquestioning faith in what God said. This was a humanistic, self-reliant righteousness that was of no more value than "filthy rags" (see Isaiah 64:6). In contrast to this, Abel trusted in what God required, offered the blood sacrifice, and his offering was accepted by God.

Not only did Cain's humanism cause inappropriate selfreliance, it also nurtured the sinful desire that ruled him. God said, "If you do well, will you not be accepted? And if you do not do well, sin lies at the door. And its desire is for you, but you should rule over it" (Gen. 4:7). His angry, jealous passion was driven by his worship of self. As he saw it, his brother's sacrifice had preempted his. This was an assault on the one Cain had enthroned; namely, himself. Therefore, the angry, hateful passion that he felt toward his brother seemed justifiable. This produced murder, one of the works of the lust of the flesh listed in Galatians 5.

Cain's humanism caused him to reject God, disobey Him and commit murder. This destroyed any hope that he may have held of being accepted by God. In contrast, Abel exercised his faith toward God's prescribed method of being accepted. This hope, involving the shedding of blood, pointed to the coming sin offering that would validate all the animal sacrifices made by faith and atone for all penitent people from then on.

The Faith of Enoch

"By faith Enoch was taken away so that he did not see death, 'and was not found because God had translated him'; for before he was taken he had this testimony, that he pleased God" (Heb. 11:5).

Enoch consistently walked in harmony with God. Jude 14–15 shows that Enoch preached to those of his time about "judgment" coming on the "ungodly." So he obviously had a clear understanding of God's way of truth. Most of the rest of the world was distracted, disinterested, and uncomprehending relative to the ways of God. Consequently, people were rapidly going in the direction of the hopeless degradation that is seen two generations later in Noah's time. Evidently, Enoch's spiritual relationship with God became so complete that it lifted him out of natural life—"God took him" (see Genesis 5:24).

Enoch was the most outstanding of those who first "began to call on the name of the LORD" (Gen. 4:26) after sin came into the world. The question for us is, Are we godly examples to our world because we are living close to God?

Enoch received the hope of eternal salvation as a result of his faith in God. His solid belief in God caused him to walk in close, trustful proximity to God. This faith-having-come-tomaturity was the confident hope he experienced. He lived this godly life against the background of the careless, humanistic, God-ignoring society of his time.

The Faith of Noah

Hebrews 11:7 tells us that, "By faith Noah, being divinely warned of things not yet seen, moved with godly fear, prepared an ark for the saving of his household, by which he condemned the world and became heir of the righteousness which is according to faith."

After sin came into the world, the general population continued to degenerate. "Then the LORD saw that the wickedness of man was great in the earth, and that every intent of the thoughts of his heart was only evil continually" (Gen. 6:5).

But Noah's thoughts were on God instead of on evil distractions because he feared the consequences of ignoring God's way. Therefore, he was in touch with God's plans for his generation and the requirements to be met for God's protection.

The question for us is, Are we in touch with what God is trying to do in our generation? Or are we only in touch with God's plans for a past generation? Are we operating in an outof-date mode? The timeless truths of God's Word must be applied to our lives in keeping with the situation of this time. For example, to teach that we should expect no greater turning to God from our preaching than Noah did would be misapplying God's timeless truth. But to teach that God is expecting us to have a much greater effect on our generation than Noah did because of the spiritual advantages that God has given us is to be in touch with God's intentions for our time. God intends for us to be His instruments in causing a great turning to God.

Because Noah was spiritually alert to God's plans for his time, God was able to reveal the concept of the covenant to him. God said, "I will establish My covenant with you," (see Genesis 6:18). The covenant related directly to God's way. It involved the understanding that God would protect Noah and his family if he would trustingly walk in God's way. By entering into the covenant with God, Noah "became heir of the righteousness which is according to faith" (Heb. 11:7).

The covenant was affirmed in the hope that was provided by the promise of the rainbow, that there would never be another such flood. This assurance was necessary to thrust Noah and his family back into normal life in the face of the destruction caused by the flood. Noah exercised the faith he received through making a covenant with God and focusing his thoughts on the hope of protecting his family. Through this faith he also became heir to the hope of righteousness that was to be fulfilled in Christ. He did this against the background of those who forgot God because their minds were filled with evil thoughts continually (see Genesis 6:5).

The Faith of Abraham

"By faith Abraham obeyed when he was called to go out to the place which he would receive as an inheritance. And he went out, not knowing where he was going. By faith he sojourned in the land of promise as in a foreign country, dwelling in tents with Isaac and Jacob, the heirs with him of the same promise; for he waited for the city which has foundations, whose builder and maker is God" (Heb. 11:8–10).

Abraham was focused more on the hope of God's blessings for future generations than on his own personal comfort. For this reason, he was willing to follow a life separated unto God while not knowing where God would lead him or when he would arrive at his destination. Therefore God could establish His covenant with Abraham and enable him to command his children after him (see Genesis 18:19).

After arriving in Canaan, Abraham remained contented to live in tents because he had the faith to understand that God was developing, through his life, the path of the way to the "city which has foundations, whose builder and maker is God" (Heb. 11:10). Thus he maintained the hope of inheriting God's promise and showing his descendants the way to inheriting the same promise. How important is the training of our children to us? Is the pursuit of comfort and financial security more important to us than perpetuating godliness in our children and grandchildren and studying how to do this?

Scripture tells us, "By faith Abraham, when he was tested, offered up Isaac, and he who had received the promises offered up his only begotten son, of whom it was said, 'In Isaac your seed shall be called,' accounting that God was able to raise him up, even from the dead, from which he also received him in a figurative sense" (Heb. 11:17–19).

The offering of Isaac would seem to be the very thing that would destroy the fulfillment of God's covenant promise, yet Abraham kept his faith in God's way in spite of the apparent contradiction. This shows the ascendancy of faith over human logic. As a result of such faith, God's blessings would go to all of Abraham's descendants who would follow God's way. These descendants would eventually include gentiles and all who would become a part of God's spiritual economy through Christ.

It is good to ask ourselves, "How strong is my faith? Does it cause me to obey God when I don't understand the reason?" Abraham's faith produced the hope of fathering a godly people and the hope of a blameless life. Thus Abraham's faith established a course for people to take that would lead them back to God. Abraham trusted God to keep His promise to bless other nations through his descendants. We greatly need this kind of faith today because so many Christians have abandoned the hope of bringing society back to God. The course that Abraham established was directly opposite to the course of the idol-worshiping people of Ur of the Chaldees. Their idol worship was leading them away from God.

The Faith of Sarah

Hebrews 11:11 tells us that "By faith Sarah herself also received strength to conceive seed, and she bore a child when she was past the age, because she judged Him faithful who had promised."

In response to Sarah's faith, God gave her a son when she was in her 90s. This was contrary to the laws of nature, so it was a miracle in the fullest sense of the word. Perhaps this was the first true miracle of the Bible after creation. Sarah learned that through believing and trusting God to overrule the laws of nature she could receive a miracle. This was against the background of others who had never believed God for miracles, except for Abraham who concurred with her faith.

Each of us would do well to ask, "Is my faith strong enough to believe God for the miracles that He wants to perform for me?"

The Faith of Isaac, Jacob, and Joseph

Here were three men who had the kind of trust in God that could make them strong contenders for the faith. Hebrews 11:20–22 says, "By faith Isaac blessed Jacob and Esau concerning things to come. By faith Jacob, when he was dying, blessed each of the sons of Joseph, and worshiped, leaning on the top of his staff. By faith Joseph, when he was dying, made mention of the departure of the children of Israel, and gave instructions concerning his bones."

This heritage was carried on by the son, grandson and great-grandson of Abraham. They all testified, when they were coming down to death's door, of their faith in God for the future. Isaac could have lost faith in God's promise when Jacob, in whom he had placed much of his hope, was gone for more than 20 years. Jacob could have concentrated on the flaws in his sons, for there were many. And Joseph could have lost hope when he was taken as a slave to Egypt. But they had patient faith.

Instead of letting the wickedness of their time overwhelm them, Isaac, Jacob, and Joseph trusted God to develop the path of God's way for their lineage that would make them a blessing. Their faith was passed down through the generations and eventually provided the Messianic hope involving the coming kingdom of God. This hope became ingrained in Jewish culture as the Lord revealed through the prophets that this was to come.

The Faith of Moses

"By faith Moses, when he was born, was hidden three months by his parents, because they saw he was a beautiful child; and they were not afraid of the king's command" (Heb. 11:23). It was from his parents' faith that Moses received the understanding of his own faith. He not only owed his very existence to his parent's courageous act in defying the king's commandment, he also owed his faith to them. The deliverance that came from Amram and Jochebed's faith showed Moses that it was best to follow God's way. Moses was taught that God always knows best; this kept him from being swayed by the worldly wisdom he later was exposed to in Egypt.

By this faith, "Moses, when he became of age, refused to be called the son of Pharaoh's daughter, choosing rather to suffer affliction with the people of God than to enjoy the passing pleasures of sin, esteeming the reproach of Christ greater riches than the treasures in Egypt; for he looked to the reward. By faith he forsook Egypt, not fearing the wrath of the king; for he endured as seeing Him who is invisible. By faith he kept the Passover and the sprinkling of blood, lest he who destroyed the firstborn should touch them. By faith they passed through the Red Sea as by dry land, whereas the Egyptians, attempting to do so, were drowned" (Heb. 11:24–29).

Moses suffered in many ways. First he was torn from his family to live with the Egyptians. Then, after he had probably grown accustomed to the privileges of the palace, he suffered banishment from it to the backside of the Median desert for 40 years. Finally, he was called (in his words) to "carry" the Israelites in his "bosom, as a guardian carries a nursing child" (see Numbers 11:12). The trials of this responsibility caused him to be denied the Promised Land.

Moses' willingness to suffer came from the same faithunderstanding that the "reproach of Christ" held riches worth suffering for. He had a clear sense of value. He realized that unless his nation could be delivered from Egypt there would be no chance of perpetuating the hope of becoming a mighty nation for God. For this reason, he chose to "suffer affliction with the people of God" rather "than to enjoy the passing pleasures of sin." Also incorporated into his hope of deliverance from Egypt was the hope of deliverance from sin. He kept the Passover and the sprinkling of blood. Both spoke of deliverance from sin.

Moses' faith in God's way was so great that he willingly accepted the suffering that was necessary to embrace the hope of deliverance from Egypt, and from sin. This confident faith was against the background of the majority of the Israelites' constant complaining about the hardships of following God to the Promised Land. **The Faith of Rahab**

Rahab had faith enough to trust God for deliverance. "By faith the harlot Rahab did not perish with those who did not believe, when she had received the spies with peace" (Heb. 11:31).

Rahab is an example of the gentiles being led out of darkness to hope in God. She simply believed God's word and trusted and obeyed. Therefore, she was saved while the other people went down with the falling walls.

The Faith of Others

Many others had the faith to do great exploits for God:
> And what more shall I say? For the time would fail me to tell of Gideon and Barak and Samson and Jephthah, also of David and Samuel and the prophets: who through faith subdued kingdoms, worked righteousness, obtained promises, stopped the mouths of lions, quenched the violence of fire, escaped the edge of the sword, out of weakness made strong, became valiant in battle, turned to flight the armies of the aliens. Women received their dead raised to life again. And others were tortured, not accepting deliverance, that they might obtain a better resurrection. Still others had trial of mockings and scourgings, yes, and of chains and imprisonment. They were stoned, they were sawn in two, were tempted, were

slain with the sword. They wandered about in sheepskins and goatskins, being destitute, afflicted, tormented— of whom the world was not worthy. They wandered in deserts and mountains, in dens and caves of the earth. And all these, having obtained a good testimony through faith, did not receive the promise, God having provided something better for us, that they should not be made perfect apart from us (Heb. 11:32–40).

In Abel we see the faith of total reliance on God and His instructions for personal salvation, which constituted faith in a sin offering. Later on, in God's plan, this faith would become the foundation of faith in Christ for salvation. In Enoch we see the faith to consistently live for God. This faith would be developed and amplified in all who would trust God for salvation and tenaciously remain true to Him through trials and tribulations.

In Noah we see the faith to be conscious of God's guidance and the kind of godly fear to act accordingly. Later, this kind of faith would be demonstrated in Joseph's divinely guided acts to protect the Christ child from those who wanted to kill him. It would be sounded in John the Baptist's call to flee from the wrath to come. It would be seen in Peter and Paul and in the other apostles' burning desire to lead people to Christ. The acts of scores of other New Testament Christians would also show this keen awareness of God's guidance and a strong desire, intensified by godly fear, to obey Him.

In Abraham we see the faith needed to establish a course for people to take; namely, the path of God's way that would lead society back to God. This faith would carry on in the many who would become aware that God intended to drastically change the world, even though others would act as though God's salvation program existed only for their small circle. Certainly those who would be filled with the Holy

Spirit on the day of Pentecost were going to see the big picture. Peter would stand up and declare that it was God's time to pour out His Spirit and perpetuate earthshaking events according to prophecy, causing 3,000 to be added to the church.

In Sarah we see the faith needed for miracles. This kind of faith would be further developed as God performed great miracles through Moses, Elijah, and Elisha. It would come into full bloom through Christ's miracles and those of His apostles. In Isaac, Jacob, and Joseph we see faith for contending for the faith in God's way and perpetuating it from generation to generation.

In Moses and his parents we see the faith for courageous suffering to obtain deliverance from those situations that bar people and society from serving God. This faith would be amplified in people like Paul, the great missionary, and in others of the church who would suffer persecution. In Rahab we see an example of the simple faith for obtaining salvation on the part of those who were outside of the commonwealth of Israel. This faith would explode into great proportions in the many gentiles who would turn to Christ. In fact, the New Testament church would eventually be populated largely by gentiles.

In the others mentioned we see the faith needed to accomplish whatever exploits God asked them to do. This kind of faith would be amplified collectively in God's future servants when they took on the challenge of conquering the world for Christ.

It took all of these building blocks of faith to complete the way that led to the level of spiritual conquest that was yet to come through Christ. This was in sharp contrast to the ungodly masses that lost their way and left no righteous path for others to follow.

The Old Testament people were not perfect. The New Testament Christian community would be needed to fully develop the spiritual conquest that started in the Old Testament. This would happen through the victory that was to be won on the cross. Only through Christ's atonement would God's way become complete.

From these examples of faith we can witness faith producing hope. The underlying commentary on all of these lives is that they excelled in their exercise of faith. Their faith was developed as it was "revealed from faith to faith" (see Romans 1:17); i.e., the faith of Abraham was revealed to Isaac, Isaac's faith was revealed to Jacob, and so on. This faith was the development of strong beliefs that matured into trust and built a monument of hope in what was to happen in the New Testament. In the future, as recorded in the book of Acts, God's program would come to be known as "the Way." This is the way that Christians take today, and the path that they take in doing so continues to have an influence on the faith of future generations.

The faith given by God the Father restored the understanding capacity of the intellect from the hardened, uncomprehending road soil seen in the parable of the sower into good soil capable of having faith in the way. Therefore, truth in the form of faith helps the heart to answer the question, "Where should I focus my faith?" It answers with spiritual understanding, "Plug your faith, the foundation of hope, into God and His way of truth."

CHAPTER 6 Love Portrayed, Love Engaged

The captain of a ship (thinking in terms of old sailing vessels) will be greatly loved by the sailors of his crew if he finds a way to show unconditional love to them. Then he will have their loyalty to stave off any possible mutiny. The captain must not only love, he must find a way to show it. The ultimate demonstration of God's love would involve sending His son to earth. This act would show that God the Father loved enough to send His only Son. God's love would also be manifest in the character of Jesus as He healed the sick, forgave sin, rebuked hypocrisy, defended the weak, and refused political advantage. The climax of God's demonstration of love would be Jesus Christ dying on the cross for all sinners even for those who crucified Him.

The time had come! The "Most Holy" was already on the earth. He was the God-Man who would "make reconciliation for iniquity" and "bring in everlasting righteousness" (see Daniel 9:24). Jesus was about 30 years old when John the Baptist proclaimed Him Messiah. Suddenly He appeared where John was preaching. Seeing Him, John cried out, "This was He of whom I said, 'He who comes after me is preferred before me, for He was before me.' And of His fullness we have all received, and grace for grace. For the law was given through Moses, but grace and truth came through Jesus Christ. No one has seen God at any time. The only begotten Son, who is in the bosom of the Father, He has declared Him" (John 1:15–18).

Jesus was the very embodiment of truth and grace in that He was the manifestation of God's love-nature. His coming was not the first time that love had been portrayed. The Old Testament had presented the love-commandments that Jesus would declare to be the greatest of all the commandments. In Deuteronomy 6:5, we read, "You shall love the LORD your God with all your heart, with all your soul, and with all your might." And in Leviticus 19:18 we read, "You shall not take vengeance, nor bear any grudge against the children of your people, but you shall love your neighbor as yourself: I am the LORD."

In the Ten Commandments, the first four are about love for God and the last six are about love for other people. Yet the conscience of the Jews had been programmed primarily by the legal aspects of the Ten Commandments rather than by the love-spirit they incorporated. Most of the Old Testament people did not have a close heart-relationship with God (see Matthew 15:8 and Mark 7:6), though some, like the people seen in Hebrews 11, approached a close relationship with God.

Love, referring to the love of God, is distinguishable from mere human love. It is God's nature made known in Christ that loves what God loves and hates what He hates. Love determines to act in character with God's will.

Love is the understanding of God's nature made known in Christ. It is from this revelatory perspective that we come to know love as unmotivated and unmanipulated, unconditional and unlimited. Such love is not a matter of feeling, which cannot be commanded, but of commitment and action. It is at the farthest pole from sentimentality and is related to the Old Testament word for "covenant love" or "steadfast love" (*hesed*).[33] Therefore, the Christlike kind that God demands is "love as a choice based on esteem and approbation as opposed to sensory affection and sentimentality."[34]

Faith is continually in the process of being exercised in hope through love. It can function only through the power of love (see Galatians 5:6). Thus faith prevails in producing hope through love. A humanistic faith that operates from a selfish incentive is not the faith that God offers. Only the faith that operates from the incentive of Christlike love is Christian faith. Love is the force that drives the processing of faith into hope. For this reason it is the greatest of faith, hope, and love (see 1 Corinthians 13:13).

We can illustrate how love drives the processing of faith into hope by expanding on our nautical, ship-sailing simile: Initially a person must have some degree of love (desire) for sailing to even have the incentive to exercise faith in the captain and become a sailor of the crew. Otherwise, the wouldbe sailor would not even consider sailing. Likewise, love (desire) for what God has to offer motivates a person to place faith in Captain Jesus when he first trusts Jesus as Savior. Therefore, a certain amount of love is present with the first step of faith for salvation. However, our sailing simile can teach us more: The sailors continue to develop love for the captain and the voyage as they engage in their duties of sailing. This gives them added incentive to exercise faith towards the hope of fulfilling their mission. Likewise, the love that develops in our Christian walk with Christ gives us

---

[33] *The New Interpreter's Bible* vol. 8 (Nashville: Abingdon Press, (1969), 425.
[34] The Zondervan Pictorial Encyclopedia of the Bible (Grand Rapids: Zondervan Publishing House, 1980), 990, 1st col.

incentive to continue to exercise faith toward producing hope in God

---

and all He has to offer. This is why the Bible says "Now hope does not disappoint, because the love of God has been poured out in our hearts by the Holy Spirit who was given to us" (Rom 5:5).

Through Jesus' ministry here on earth, and through His death, love was effectively demonstrated (see Romans 5:8). Love caused Him to leave His Heavenly glory and condescend to live among people. In healing the sick, denouncing hypocrisy and forgiving sin, Jesus was motivated by love. Through the power of love He maintained His strength of purpose to endure the agony of the cross. John says, "God is love" (1 John 4:8). The cutting edge of Christ's ministry is love.

The New Covenant

God's truth was revealed in the Old Testament covenant, but in Christ the old covenant was fulfilled and a new covenant was established. "In that He says, 'A new covenant,' He has made the first obsolete. Now what is becoming obsolete and growing old is ready to vanish away" (Heb. 8:13). The new covenant is based on love, for in addition to emphasizing the two great commands of love (see Matthew 22:37–39), Jesus taught, "As the Father loved Me, I also have loved you; abide in My love. If you keep My commandments, you will abide in My love, just as I have kept My Father's commandments and abide in His love" (John 15:9–10). He also taught His disciples to love each other. Jesus said, "A new commandment I give to you, that you love one another; as I have loved you, that you also love one another. By this all will know that you are My disciples, if you have love for one another" (John 13:34–35).

Furthermore, Jesus commanded His people to love all humankind: "You have heard that it was said, 'You shall love your neighbor and hate your enemy.' But I say to you, love your enemies, bless those who curse you, do good to those who hate you, and pray for those who spitefully use you and persecute you, that you may be sons of your Father in heaven; for He makes His sun rise on the evil and on the good, and sends rain on the just and on the unjust" (Matt. 5:43–44).

In the Old Testament, the concept of love (*hesed*) was involved in the covenant. God contended with Israel for turning from loving Him to whoring after other gods. Yet the covenant was not so clearly understood to be a covenant of love as it is in the New Testament. The teaching that one should hate an enemy illustrates this (see Matthew 5:43). Also, the fact that Jeremiah prophesied, "I will put My law in their minds, and write it on their hearts" (Jer. 31:33), showed that a high level of love, especially loving God's law, or truth, was something that for the most part had not yet come. This high level of love was to be revealed in Christ, especially in the sacrifice of Himself as a sin offering.

We are reminded that the willingness of Jesus to die in our place was love's acknowledgment of the truth that we needed a Savior. Therefore, His offering was love's ultimate act of truth—the truth that "Christ died for the ungodly" (see Romans 5:6). This provision of truth was God's ultimate demonstration of love's identity with truth. His atonement was the ultimate truth-reality.

In saying "you shall love the LORD your God with all your heart, with all your soul, with all your mind, and with all your strength" (Matt. 22:37; Mark 12:30; Luke 10:27), Jesus was stating that mankind had a conscious capacity for love.

Specifically, the faculties named had the capacity to love. Therefore, in order to understand God's development of love in people, we must study these faculties.

This teaching shows that the human personality is broader than the heart. So we will now broaden our study to include the soul and the mind. Jesus also mentioned "strength" in connection with love. But we understand "strength" to be the power of the three faculties to love rather than a faculty distinguishable from the heart, the soul, and the mind. The heart, soul, and mind constitute the inner person.

We know that the heart is central to spiritual awareness and functions in terms of faith, love, and hope through its three faculties: the intellect, the will, and the conscience. Now we need to explore how the heart relates to the rest of the inner person—the soul and the mind.

The Functions of the Heart, Soul, and Mind

In the Bible, the references to the heart are much more numerous than the references to either the soul or the mind. The heart is mentioned 545 times; the soul, 125 times; and the mind, 114 times. Taking into consideration all of these references with a view to Greek and Hebrew cultural usage of the terms, we find their respective functions.

Emotions expressed by "longing," "rejoicing," "grief," "bitterness," "anguish," "sorrow," "yearning," and "joy"—are attributed both to the heart and the soul. However, more contemplative functions are attributed only to the heart.

The heart is capable of "thought" and "cunning"; it "ponders," and can be "honest" or "deceitful" and "deluded." The heart also exercises willpower. Accordingly, it can be "steadfast" or characterized by "stubbornness." It can have self-conscious attitudes such as: "envy," "arrogance," "pride," or "humility." The heart can also be "pure" and "upright," or "sick" and "wicked," etc. Its intuitiveness is seen in its "discerning" and "praying."

A high capability for knowledge and reason is attributed to the mind in most of the Bible references to the heart. It is important to note that the mind shares the intellect and conscience with the heart. This means that we perceive both the heart and the mind as having understanding as well as instinctive, intuitive faculties. However, it seems quite obvious that the collective functions of the heart are much more intuitive than are the collective functions of the mind. The mind is far more rational; it is not as influenced as the heart by the desires of the will. In the mind, the intellect seems to be dominant over the conscience.

When it comes to the mind, the intellect is its first faculty to respond to an encounter with God or evil. The response takes the form of rational spiritual understanding—creating faith. This faith-understanding then produces hope. Hope is a signal to the conscience to appraise value in God, or value in rejecting the evil that has been encountered.

The heart is signaled via the intellect and via the conscience since these faculties are also the faculties of the heart. This signaling now causes the heart to respond in desire. This desire is the determined passion of the will—expressing the understanding of the intellect and the appraisal of value of the conscience—which stimulates the mind to signal the body via the brain to act righteously.

At times the encounter with God or evil is subtle and sudden, which tends to cause the heart to respond without first being signaled by the mind. This is an intuitive valueresponse. The hope that is present in the conscience is a value judgment calling for the value-response. This could be a subconscious activity.

Psychologist Thomas H. Metros gives an interesting definition of the mind in introducing his book, *The Human Mind*. He says, "A useful definition of the mind is: the organized totality or system of all mental processes or psychic activities of an individual."[35]

Volition, in conjunction with desire, extends beyond the mind. We perceive this function happening in the heart even though mind activity is involved. Certainly the mind has a bearing on desire-strengthened volition; i.e., "willing mind" (see 2 Corinthians 8:12). But its function is primarily a function of the heart.

Metros also recognizes, along with other psychologists, that the mind is not limited to the brain, showing that they recognize the mind to be a cognitive process that extends the personality beyond the merely biological.[36]

Various Scriptures speak of spiritual functions metaphorically in terms of the five physical senses: "Oh, taste and see that the LORD is good" (Ps. 34:8). "You have become dull of hearing" (Heb. 5:11). "Having eyes, do you not see? And having ears, do you not hear?" (Mark 8:18). "Do not touch what is unclean" (2 Cor. 6:17). Such expressions seem to hint that the structure of the outer person can give us a picture of the inner person. Therefore, we will look at the

---

[35] Metros, *The Human Mind* (New York/ London/Toronto/Sydney: Franklin Watts, 1990), 8.
[36] Ibid. 89.

faculties and functions of the outer person for some working hypotheses to understand the inner person:

---

1. The soul is the general term for the inner person, as the body is the general term for the outer person. Therefore, we can view the soul as the inner body.
2. The heart of the inner person is central to the inner person and corresponds to the physical heart in that it is central to the outer person.
3. The mind of the inner person has capacity for spiritual knowledge and reasoning and corresponds to the brain of the outer person in that the brain obviously has much the same capabilities, though it does not have the capacity for spiritual discernment that the mind has. These hypotheses can be tested in observing how the interaction of spiritual faculties corresponds to interaction of the physical faculties.

The physical heart is kept in motion by electrical impulses from the brain. Yet the heart pumps blood through the brain to provide life to it. Thus the heart has its own distinctive pumping functions in keeping with its design, and the brain also has its own distinctive impulse-sending functions in terms of its design. Yet the two interact and support one another in accomplishing their specific chores. Likewise, the heart of the inner person, in keeping with its design, receives impulses from the mind that signal it to respond to God, while the feelings of the heart, that are in keeping with its design, stimulate the mind to be alive to the spiritual truths that cause it to send these impulses. This spiritual interaction keeps the soul alive to God as the physical interaction of the faculties (or organs) of the body keep it alive to the physical world.

In the Bible, the term "soul" can have two different meanings. It can denote the entire inner person or it can denote that part of the inner person that is distinct from the heart and mind. According to this later usage, Jesus says, "You shall love the Lord your God with all your heart, with all your soul, with all your mind" (see Mark 12:30). Here again these different meanings can be illustrated in the way the terms for the outer faculties are commonly used. It is common to speak of the heart, brain, and body in distinguishing each from the other. Yet the heart and brain are normally thought to be included when one refers only to the body. Accordingly, soul can refer to the entire inner person or it can refer to the inner person as distinct from the heart and mind.

The spirit encompasses the whole personality. The soul includes the heart and mind. The heart and mind share the intellect and conscience, but the mind is distinct from the will. The mind and the body share the brain.

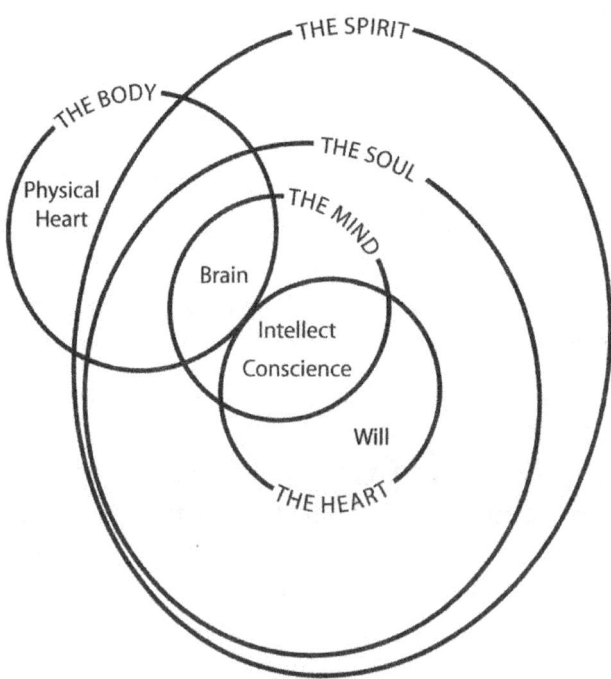

The soul can express itself through the body, and through the body it experiences the natural world. However, the soul also has another way of expressing itself and having experiences. This is through the human spirit. People can experience God and commune with Him in the spirit realm, for "God is Spirit" (see John 4:24). Thus the soul can have both a spiritual orientation and a sensory orientation.[37] If the soul is primarily oriented to the natural, biological world, it is inclined to be sensual. On the other hand, if it's primarily

---

[37] *The Expositors Bible Commentary* vol. 11, shows that Paul's training involved the teaching that the "soul (psyche) is the sphere of man's will and emotions. Here is true center of personality. It gives him a selfconsciousness that relates to the physical world through the body and to God through the spirit." [Grand Rapids: Zondervan Publishing House, 1978], 295.

orientated to the spiritual world, it is inclined to be spiritual.[38] The soul cannot be free from bodily interaction with earthly life, nor would it be desirable. Yet the soul is designed to have a greater orientation to the spirit than to the body.

The spiritual orientation is developed through worship. Jesus said, "God is Spirit, and those who worship Him must worship in spirit and truth" (see John 4:24). Love contains a strong urge to worship God, as perverted-love sensualism contains the strong inclination to worship the god-self. The more one worships God, the more he is fascinated with God and the more godly and spiritual he becomes. Likewise, the more one worships self, the more self-centered and sensual he becomes. Satan and his demons bring a type of spirituality to this self-worship because they are spirits. Yet this is not a true spirituality because it is oriented to the sensual and material.

Those who teach a gospel that majors on material prosperity demonstrate that their worship is being influenced by the sensual and material. Materialism is a false hope, but it is an infinitely greater falsehood to turn spiritual hope into materialistic hope by applying the Bible's promises of spiritual prosperity to mere material prosperity. Real hope is to be found in the spiritual and the eternal. From this hope, one gains the material prosperity that God wills. "Seek first the kingdom of God and His righteousness, and all these things shall be added to you" (Matt. 6:33).

---

[38] Psychologist Steven Reiss recognizes both the spiritual orientation and the biological orientation... "We seek feel-good happiness because we are biological beings and value-based happiness because we are spiritual beings."

A person is spiritually enabled, through faith, to lay hold of his hope by the power of love's worship. Worship is essentially to do homage or make obeisance to God "in sprit and truth" (see John 4:23). It is the concentrated meditation on God's exalted greatness. Thus minds discover reasons to love God and hearts to contemplate His grandeur, which fills souls with emotion toward Him. With this abundant consciousness, the human spirit is brought into harmony with God, which increases faith, love, and hope.

The Sanctifying Process of Love

Agape is widely celebrated by scholars to be the Greek noun describing the love Christ taught and exemplified. It is defined as "a love which is awakened by a sense of value in its object—a love of esteem and approbation." (The verb is *agapao*). This love is to be distinguished from *phileo*, a love of tender affection, "which consists of the glow of the heart kindled by the perception of that in the object which affords us pleasure."[39] It is also to be distinguished from *eros,* which is sexual love. *Agape* is "love as a choice." Stated another way, it is a process of choosing in character with God's will. It involves the will more than the emotions.[40]

Apparently, *agape* is the closest Greek word to the Hebrew word *hesed*, which is defined as "covenant love" or "steadfast love." Therefore, *agape* and *hesed* are the best words of the original languages for the love that Jesus portrayed—the love of God. Yet no one or two words can adequately convey a

---

[39] Quotes on *agape* and *phileo* love taken from *Word Studies in the Greek New Testament,* vol. 3, Kenneth Wuest, (Grand Rapids: Wm. B. Eerdmans Publishing company, 1983), 60–62.

[40] *The Zondervan Pictorial Encyclopedia of the Bible* (Grand Rapids: Zondervan Publishing House, 1980), 990, 1st col.

revelation of the love of God. Only the manifest character of Christ can portray this love that is "'unmotivated and unmanipulated, unconditional and unlimited,' love that 'is not a matter of feeling, which cannot be commanded in any case, but of commitment and action,' such that it is 'the farthest pole from sentimentality.'"[41]

This love is the love that comes to those who yield to God. In the Bible it is often referred to as the "love of God" (see Luke 11:42, John 5:42, Romans 5:5, Romans 8:39, 2 Corinthians13:14, 2 Thessalonians 3:5, Titus 3:4, 1 John 2:5, 1 John 3:17, 1 John 4:9, 1 John 5:3, and Jude 21).

This love, and the accompanying faith and hope, are Godgiven dynamics, not mere human exercises. Therefore, it would appear that sanctification is accomplished in the dynamic processes that are faith, love, and hope as the Spirit applies truth to hearts by grace through faith. Much of this

---

happens progressively. Basically, sanctification is accomplished in love. Love "believes all things" and "hopes all things" (see 1 Corinthians 13:7). Therefore, any expression of love is also an expression of faith and hope. Apart from faith and hope, love is not love. This is an important truth that many have missed who stress the love-factor in sanctification.

Some may object to the idea that faith, love, and hope are sanctifying processes, saying that sanctification is consecration to God and cleansing from sinful tendencies. Yet by their nature, faith, love, and hope appear to do both. Faith consecrates people to trust in God and cleanses them of

---

[41] *The New Interpreter's Bible*, vol. 8, (Nashville: Abingdon Press, 1969), 425.

prideful self-reliance. Love cleanses all contrary loves. It crowds out sinful or unholy love just as a man's exclusive love for his wife crowds out love for other women. John Wesley's view on this has been described as "love expelling sin." Hope in God consecrates people to enthusiasm for God and cleanses them of enthusiasm for those things that do not have value for building and establishing God's kingdom.

It is important to understand that our relationship with God begins with faith, but as the basic Christian exercise of faithproducing-hope-through-the-power-of-love takes place, love becomes the dominant dynamic. But love does not operate alone; it incorporates faith and hope. Therefore, with all the above considered, love, with faith and hope incorporated, seems to form the essence of sanctification.

However, sanctification is not a mere human exercise. It is a Calvary-provided application of grace that is received through faith. As it is received, progressive-conditioning effects begin to take place in the Christian's life. The process of sanctification is begun in the heart by the "washing of regeneration" that happens in justification (see Titus 3:5–7). Subsequently, it results in full surrender to God involving a reckoning of oneself "dead indeed to sin, but alive to God in Christ Jesus our Lord" (Rom. 6:11). At this point all love for sin, the essence of which is self-centeredness, must die that one might become alive to a God-orientation. This releases one to a highly productive Christian life. Paul spoke of this when he said, "May the God of peace Himself sanctify you completely" (1 Thess. 5:23).

The aorist Greek verb for "sanctify" shows point of action; it is a point-in-time when sanctification becomes complete. The same verb is used in Jesus' prayer, "Sanctify them through Your truth. Your word is truth" (John 17:17), and in the expression to the Hebrews, "That He might sanctify the people with His own blood" (Heb. 13:12). Sanctification thus becomes complete, or entire, in the sense that all unholy love, or love for sin, is dead and therefore no willful, voluntary resistance to God remains. Yet, entirely sanctified people have need for spiritual growth; they must continue to become more and more like Christ.

It is important to emphasize that Christ's blood (indicative of His death) is the grounds for God's offer of sanctification and justification. As animals were offered outside the camp in the Old Testament on the Day of Atonement, Jesus shed His blood and offered himself for sin outside the gate of Jerusalem. The blood is the ground for sanctification, while the word of God is the communication of sanctification (see John 17:17). This grace-applied truth happens in the dynamic process of love that incorporates faith and hope. With these realities stated in this paragraph in mind, let us put everything in clear perspective:

1. Christ's shed blood is the grounds for sanctification.
2. Grace offers sanctification.
3. God's Word is the communication of sanctification.
4. Love, incorporating faith and hope, is the dynamic process of sanctification.

We can have an ever-developing relationship with God. The faith-love-hope relationship with God is ever developing. Love comes to the heart with the initial faith that is received from God as it (faith) is exercised into the hope of salvation. This love causes the will to continually choose more of God, who keeps coming and bringing more faith. The recipient exercises this faith, and love increases. This increase in love produces more hope, because faith is always in the process of producing hope through the power of love. As hope floods the heart, love responds with greater enthusiasm for God, which stimulates faith to start the process all over again. Thus the three—faith, love, and hope—are continually increasing and intensifying in the healthy, normal Christian causing an everincreasing upward spiral reach for God.

Those who believe in Christ desire to obey "the truth" as opposed to being "self-seeking" (see Romans 2:8). The desire to obey is a sanctifying love-process that produces inner, ethical righteousness. Those who argue that we cannot have a change of heart, or inner ethical righteousness, have not properly reckoned with Paul's teaching on the carnal mind and the flesh:

> There is therefore now no condemnation to those who are in Christ Jesus, who do not walk according to the flesh, but according to the Spirit. For the law of the Spirit of life in Christ Jesus has made me free from the law of sin and death. For what the law could not do in that it was weak through the flesh, God did by sending His own Son in the likeness of sinful flesh, on account of sin: He condemned sin in the flesh, that the righteous requirement of the law might be fulfilled in us who do not walk according to the flesh but according to the Spirit. For those who live according to the flesh set their minds on the things of the flesh, but those who live according to the Spirit, the things of the Spirit. For to be carnally minded is death, but to be spiritually minded is life and peace. Because the carnal mind is enmity against God; for it is not subject to the law of God, nor indeed can be. So then, those who are in the flesh cannot please God. But you are not in the flesh but in the Spirit, if indeed the Spirit of God dwells in you. Now if anyone does not have the Spirit of Christ, he is not His. And if Christ is in you, the body is dead because of sin, but the Spirit is life because of righteousness (Rom. 8:1–10).

Because some have "set their minds on the things of the Spirit," they are no longer "carnally minded," but "spiritually minded." In the words of the Holman Christian Standard Bible, they have the "mind-set of the Spirit" instead of the "mind-set of the flesh" (Rom. 8:6). This is a change in character involving a choice to love what God loves. By contrast, the "carnal mind" is a self-centered perspective.

The flesh is not the same as the carnal mind, but it is related. "The flesh," as it is used in this chapter, is the life lived apart from God. It is the product of the perspective and agenda of the carnal mind, or the mind-set of the flesh. However, a person acts with the Spirit when he first trusts Christ as his Savior. Therefore, he is no longer in the flesh. But, as with the Corinthian Christians, the newly converted heart struggles with some of the old carnal perspective (see 1 Corinthians 3:3). For this reason, the godly love in the Christian needs to be perfected (see 1 John 4:18) to strengthen the will against the old carnal perspective.

The old man that is to be crucified and put off (see Romans 6:6, Ephesians 4:22) includes both the flesh and the carnal mind.

Jesus was the very embodiment of love; His ministry on earth was centered in love. Love, the very nature of God, was portrayed in His earthly life and ministry. Jesus imparts to us this love of God whereby we are commanded to love with our conscious faculties: heart, mind, and entire soul. This love drives the fundamental act of faith producing hope through love. Also, this love incorporates faith and hope to produce the dynamic process of sanctification, which brings one to a point of becoming fully committed to living in the Spirit instead of apart from God in the flesh. From this point on, love continues to grow in intensity.

The love made known in Christ restores the volitional capacity of the will into the good soil of love for God and the truth. Therefore, truth in the form of love causes the heart to answer the question, "Where should I focus my capacity for love?" It answers in the spirit of great, sanctified determination, "I choose to love God and His truth, for by thus directing my love, I plug-in to God powerful capacity to love."

Plugged-in to the Dynamic Word

CHAPTER 7 Hope Fulfilled

As the winds of the Holy Spirit fill our sails of conscience with the hope of effectively sailing against the contrary winds of Satan's kingdom we gain great spiritual momentum. Scripture speaks often of hope. For example, in Romans 5:13 we read, "Now may the God of hope fill you with all joy and peace in believing, that you may abound in hope by the power of the Holy Spirit."

The Spirit directly empowers us, but He also enables us through the works of Satan. As head winds propel a sailing vessel against those very winds by proper adjustment of the sails, the Holy Spirit empowers us to gain spiritual momentum by the very winds of evil that are intended to reverse our course. The hate that Satan's kingdom directs toward us intensives our prayers for more "love-poured-out- in-ourhearts by the Holy Spirit" (see Romans 5:5). And this love strengthens our wills with determination to fend-off the enemy cannonballs (thinking in terms of old battleships) of depression and ridicule with the shield of faith that produces hope.

The Holy Spirit also works through the contrary winds of Satan's persecution to inspire us. Persecution intuitively informs our sails of conscience and rationally informs our rudders of understanding that Satan knows the gospel we spread is defeating his evil cause. Thus our ship of being is propelled on the sea of life with the encouraging knowledge we are winning.

However, the Holy Spirit not only empowers the Christians, He also works on unbelievers. He directly infiltrates the world with His convicting power because He is spirit, not subject to the time and space limitations of a physical body (see John 16:8). We need more awareness of this Holy Spirit-reality to give us hope for impacting the world beyond which human Christian witness can go. By the Spirit's power, hope for the Kingdom of God to conquer the kingdom of Satan will be fulfilled.

Even though there were outstanding examples of faith in the Old Testament, generally speaking the primitive faith of that time produced a type of hope that was much more materialistic than would be expected in New Testament times. The Old Testament people were largely focused on conquering and maintaining the land of Palestine and gaining material possessions. To them, spiritual success was measured largely in how much land and how many sheep, camels, donkeys, etc., they possessed. This was true even for the faithful Abraham. Why?

Most Old Testament people did not comprehend and experience the degree of love that later became known in Christ. Because of this, their hope was a primitive, more materialistic hope. Evidently the same is true of contemporary pop religion that greatly over-emphasizes the importance of material prosperity. Faith can produce mature spiritual hope only through the power of Christlike love. Not until Jesus was able to demonstrate the nature of God in His life and death on earth was God's love adequately expressed to humankind. "God demonstrates his own love toward us, in that while we were still sinners, Christ died for us" (Rom. 5:8). And only through this manifested love, that incorporated a high level of faith and hope, was advanced spiritual conquest made possible. However, something else was still lacking; a spiritual medium was needed to convey God's love all across the world and to reveal the full significance of Christ's atonement.

This need is realized in the baptism of the Holy Spirit. As people are baptized with the power of God's love, spiritual dullness gives way to a great awareness of what God wanted to do in the world. Only through this baptism could God penetrate the inner person with His love. People's thoughts would be filled with the new level of love that Christ had provided. This was not possible before Jesus came because only He could "baptize... with the Holy Spirit and fire" (see Matthew 3:11) and provide the love that comes with such baptism.

Therefore, the faithful of the Old Testament, though "having obtained a good testimony through faith, did not receive the promise" (see Hebrews 11:39). They, along with the disciples before Pentecost, were limited. Yet even after Christ came, only the baptism of the Holy Spirit could properly apply the spiritual power He provided so that the promised land of dominion over sin could be won.

This victory first became a widespread reality at Pentecost after Christ's ascension when hearts were purified by faith (see Acts 15:9). It was through "this dispensation of the fullness of the times" (Eph 1:10a) that God would "gather together in one all things in Christ, both which are in heaven and which are on earth—in Him" (Eph. 1:10b). Through the work of the Holy Spirit not only would hearts become fully surrendered to God and be purified but also, through Him, the earth would be subdued (see Genesis 1:28). The dispensation of the Holy Spirit is about the hope provided by these benefits collectively along with the dispensations of the Father and the Son.

Through the Holy Spirit, Christ's kingdom of truth would eventually correct all falsehood—all things working contrary to truth. Some teach that the dispensation of the Holy Spirit will end in defeat like all the other so-called dispensations that they perceive in the Old Testament. In this they are fundamentally wrong. The Holy Spirit's agenda for the New Testament dispensation is one of victory. Obviously, some falsehood will remain until the end of time.

It is to be acknowledged that God gives Satan certain freedom. This is being seen in the horrible tribulation that is upon us. More Christians were martyred in the 20th century than in all the preceding 19 centuries. Satan has amassed a great army of unbelievers who are seething in rebellion. But God must allow this accumulated rebellion its opportunity of expression to fulfill His obligation to play by His own rules—rules giving people freedom to choose the wrong way. But, when God has fulfilled this obligation, He will judge the world in the great day of His wrath (see Revelation 6:17).

Yet these apocalyptic events do not make up God's primary strategy for spiritual conquest. Spiritual conquest is happening by Jesus building His church. Jesus intends for His church to be triumphant and His cause to prevail over the wickedness in society. We say this with the understanding that the Bible does predict a "falling away" (see 2 Thessalonians 2:3). But there is no indication that falling away is attributed to the end time more than to other times. Many apostasies have occurred since Paul wrote these words, so no more apostasies have to happen for this prophecy to be fulfilled. It is much easier to blame the times for the lack of spiritual revival in a particular country or locality than to put forth great effort in prayer and witness to improve the situation. It is time we quit the "cop-out" and the making of excuses and become fired up with the hope that comes when we trust God to make a difference and to help us work to make a difference.

Daniel's 70 Weeks Relative to Hope

Some have viewed the last week of the 70 weeks of years (seven years) in Daniel 9 that relate to anointing the "Most Holy" to be portraying the Antichrist of the end time. However, since the occurrence of all the weeks were necessary to anoint the Most Holy, it is difficult to understand how anyone could arrive at this conclusion. Could the coming of Christ's anointing, and His ministry here on earth, be dependent on what was to come after Him? Of course not! It is obvious that the promoters of this doctrine have not observed that all of the weeks were to occur relative to Christ's coming to earth to make reconciliation for sin. Yet this doctrine is widespread and is a major premise for the idea that this age (the church age) is destined to go down in defeat like other ages or perceived dispensations of the past.

This idea causes a lot of fear and discouragement and thus greatly militates against hope for building the kingdom of God on earth. How can we be excited about a cause that is destined to go down in defeat? Satan is happy to promote this idea because he knows that one of the best strategies of combat is to weaken the enemy with the fear that he is fighting an overwhelming force and is losing the battle. Satan tries to take away our hope by giving us a perception of fear.

It is psychologically necessary to know that the church of Jesus Christ is winning the war here on earth. This is not to suggest that all evil is going to be destroyed in the church age, but Jesus promised, "I will build My church, and the gates of Hades shall not prevail against it" (Matt. 16:18). This hope gives the necessary incentive to aggressively engage in God's work.

The appropriate interpretation of Daniel's seventieth week is that this is about Christ's short ministry on earth and the first years that followed His ascension into heaven. Christ's supreme sin-offering on the cross was what brought "an end to sacrifice and offering"—the primary event of this week (see Daniel 9:27). This week was right at seven years (one week of years) from the beginning of Christ's earthly ministry until the early church began turning to the gentiles. Therefore, this was the last "week" of years that God ministered to the world almost exclusively through the Jews. Therefore, it is reasonable to conclude that this was the last of the 70 weeks, those weeks that were "determined for your people and for your holy city," Daniel's people, the Israelites (see Daniel 9:24).

The hermeneutic of applying Daniel's 70th week to Antichrist and the end time has also supported the groundless idea that the book of Revelation is primarily about a time yet to come. Obviously some of the book is about events future to our time, but much of its prophesy has been fulfilled.

This futuristic view has given rise to much preoccupation with the timing of Christ's second coming and to the false hope of a second chance to go to heaven after this coming that is described in 1Thessalonians 4.

Our focus should be on "Do business till I come" (see Luke 19:13) and being ready at any time, rather than being preoccupied with the timing of Christ's second coming which often distracts us from the long-range planning necessary to effectively build a future for God's kingdom on earth. We make this brief reference to prophesy only to note that many modern prophetic interpretations are not based on good biblical exegesis and are destructive to our hope.

The Holy Spirit is capable of spiritually penetrating the consciousness of the inner person. He can do this without regard to time and space because He is spirit. He is not limited to communicating in an audible voice or by appearances in human flesh. He also does not have the bodily limitations that Jesus had while on this earth. Therefore, He can most effectively and efficiently deliver the salvation that Jesus provided.

The Breaking of Our Heart's Soil

The Holy Spirit "breaks-up" the "fallow ground" (see Hosea 10:12) of hearts through three areas of conviction—sin, righteousness, and judgment. Scripture says, "And when He has come, He will convict the world of sin, and of righteousness, and of judgment: of sin, because they do not believe in Me; of righteousness, because I go to My Father and you see Me no more; of judgment, because the ruler of this world is judged" (John 16:8–11). There are three areas of conviction that break up the fallow ground of hearts. They are sin-conviction, righteousness-conviction, and judgmentconviction.

Sin-conviction

Jesus said that the Holy Spirit would convict the world of sin "because they do not believe in Me," showing that sinconviction relates to unbelief. The most basic faith needed to save from sin is the faith to believe in Jesus as Savior, "for there is no other name under heaven given among men by which we must be saved" (Acts 4:12). And. "All we like sheep have gone astray; We have turned, every one, to his own way; And the Lord has laid on Him the iniquity of us all" (Isa. 53:6). Yes, "all have sinned and fall short of the glory of God" (Rom. 3:23). The Spirit has been sent to convict us of this truth so that we will become believers in the One who can save us from sin. Several kinds of unbelief exist in the world and each results in sin.

One form of unbelief is called "uninformed unbelief." Some have never heard of Jesus, so it is obvious that they do not have faith in Jesus and are still in their sin. That is not because they refuse to believe but because they have not had the opportunity to believe in the only one who can save them from their sins.

The world has another category of unbelievers, those who persist in walking a sinful path after having been exposed to the way of truth. Such persons demonstrate that they believe in their own ways as opposed to God's way. This persistent unbelief is rooted in the prideful, arrogant attitude that hardens the heart against faith. But when a person truly believes in Christ, he is inclined to act accordingly, for to truly believe in Jesus is to believe in all that He taught, including what He taught about living righteously.

Unbelief may be based on the wrong concept of sin. In the Old Testament, sin was defined primarily in terms of specific acts. Consequently, the unintentional as well as the deliberate breaking of the objective law of God was considered sin. In the New Testament, sin is defined primarily in terms of our relationship with God. "Essentially, the biblical concept of sin is a wrong relationship with God."[42] Sin can be defined thus: "Anything in thought, deed, or disposition which disrupts one's relationship with God is sin."[43]

---

[42] "Biblical Concepts of Sin," (*Wesleyan Theological Journal* Vol. 1, No.1, Spring 1966)

[43] Kenneth Kinghorn, "Biblical Concepts of Sin," (*Wesleyan Theological Journal* Vol,1, No. 1, Spring 1966)

To get a full concept of sin, we must recognize that sin has different meanings and that the context in the Bible must be considered to determine the meaning. In certain contexts the meaning is willful, voluntary sin. In others the meaning is to fall short of doing the will of God without intending to do so. This is unintentional sin in a New Testament context. In either case, the sin has a disruptive effect on our relationship with God. To have the wrong concept of sin is to not believe in the true concept of sin. When speaking of willful, voluntary sin, the apostle John says, "Whoever has been born of God does not sin, for His seed remains in him; and he cannot sin, because he has been born of God" (1 John 3:9).

Sin is lawlessness, 1 John 3:4 tells us. In 1 John 3:7 we read that "he who practices righteousness is righteous." Then 1 John 3:10 tells us that whosoever does not practice righteousness is not of God. This is willful sin, the kind of sin that is the practice of lawlessness, the opposite of practicing righteousness.

Basically, John is saying that love is the essence of the practice of righteousness. Now if we interpret the clause, "he cannot sin because he has been born of God," in the light of this context, we see that Christians cannot wander from the practice of righteousness if they love God. They can only depart from this path after their love for God has cooled off.

Also, the Bible makes it plain that Christ provided no sacrifice for the practice of willful, persistent sinning (see Hebrews 10:26–27). For we are told, "If we sin willfully after we have received the knowledge of the truth, there no longer remains a sacrifice for sins, but a certain fearful expectation of judgment, and fiery indignation which will devour the adversaries." Sin conviction is for the purpose of correcting the unbelief that allows one to believe that it is to his advantage to commit willful, voluntary sin.

When it comes to unintentional sin, Jesus is referring to the kind of sin that falls short of doing the will of God without intending to do so when He teaches His disciples to pray, "And forgive us our sins" (see Luke 11:4). Here the Lord is not referring to the willful practice of lawlessness, because people are not disciples if they are living thus. Since the Lord taught us to pray this way, we conclude that Christians need to ask forgiveness for some kinds of sin.

Also, honesty requires us to admit that we all fall short. If we fail to recognize this, it could lead us into spiritual pride that lacks the awareness of our need to constantly rely on the mercy of God and Christ's atonement for sin. This would cause a certain amount of hardness against God. The pride of life causes hardness and precludes faith in Jesus. While we recognize, as Wesley did, that sin can be a voluntary transgression of the known law of God, we should also understand that sin is falling short—anything that disrupts our relationship with God.

Falling short can be caused by a degree of unbelief, for the more a person believes in God's program and is sold on its value, the more he will strive to live it out. But if his belief is weak, his striving to perform will also be weak. This doesn't mean, however, that anything short of the absolute perfection of God is sin. Failing to perform perfectly does not necessarily disrupt our relationship with God. We should also recognize that God can enable us to faithfully follow the path of righteousness, avoiding willful sin. Sin conviction is for the kind of unbelief that produces carelessness toward striving to live out God's will.

Wrong desire, or love for sin, is also caused by unbelief. John says "Do not love the world or the things in the world. If anyone loves the world, the love of the Father is not in him" (1 John 2:15). From this we can conclude that to the extent the love of the world is in a person, to that extent he does not love God. And to the extent a person loves God, to that extent the love of the world is not in him. Therefore, to the extent the love of the world is in him and the love of God is not in him, to that extent he is sinful in his desires. Sinful desires are rooted in unbelief, for if a person truly believes in God and His way—being sold to God—he hates what is contrary to God's will. A true believer cannot desire what is contrary to the way that he believes with all of his heart. Therefore, sin conviction is also for the kind of unbelief that promotes wrong desire.

Sin is the end result of unbelief, but faith in Jesus saves people from sin. The Holy Spirit has been sent into the world to convict people of sin and to cause them to believe in their need of the Savior for deliverance from sin's dilemmas and consequences. The Spirit's sin-conviction brings the lawless to the attitude, "God, be merciful to me a sinner" (see Luke 18:13). After conversion, this attitude of dependency on the mercy of God must continue for people to maintain a clear assurance of justification (see Luke 18:14). This is the breaking-up of the unbelieving hard soil of the intellect.

Righteousness-conviction

Jesus related righteousness-conviction to the fact of His going to the Father where His disciples would "see Him no more." Beholding Jesus reveals the love that is God's nature made known in Him—"God is love" (see 1 John 4:8). Therefore, beholding Him increases love for God in the beholder.

Paul calls righteousness conviction the "ministry of righteousness" in 2 Corinthians 3:8–9 and then later in the chapter shows how Christians, "with unveiled face,"... are "beholding... the glory of the Lord," and in so doing, are being "transformed" into Christ's image. The apostle says, "But even to this day, when Moses is read, a veil lies on their heart. Nevertheless when one turns to the Lord, the veil is taken away. Now the Lord is the Spirit; and where the Spirit of the Lord is, there is liberty. But we all, with unveiled face, beholding as in a mirror the glory of the Lord, are being transformed into the same image from glory to glory, just as by the Spirit of the Lord" (2 Cor. 3:15–18).

Our understanding is unveiled by the "Spirit of the Lord" to behold Jesus (view Him as our mentor and guide) which "transforms us" into His image, or into having His righteous character of which love is the essence. Therefore, righteousness-conviction is really a love process.

We cannot behold Jesus in physical form as the people did who lived when He walked the face of this earth, but we behold Jesus through the righteousness-conviction of the Holy Spirit.

The Spirit is sent to convict of the righteousness that Jesus' character portrays. He does this by enabling people to behold Christ, which is to behold the love of God made known in Him—which love is the essence of righteousness. This keeps us from being distracted from Him by ungodly love. Beholding Jesus produces the love that breaks up the stony resistance to God caused by sensual, self-centered love.

Judgment-conviction

Jesus said that the Holy Spirit would convict the world of judgment because "the ruler of this world is judged" (see John 16:11). Because of Calvary, Satan, the arch enemy of God and the ring leader of wickedness, was brought to judgment. He was judged to have no rightful claim on eternal souls and to be deserving of eternal damnation. As a result, he was required to release those who trusted Christ's atonement for their sins. Those of the Old Testament who trusted in God for salvation in offering animal sacrifices were trusting indirectly in the atonement Christ would offer.

Because of God's promise to Adam and Eve that sin would bring death, God could not forgive sins without demanding the payment of death. Only Jesus as God could offer a life that was of sufficient quality. Only He could experience a death as serious as the death of all people. If a human being had been born into this world free of sin and had maintained his sinless state, the giving of his life could have been grounds for the atonement of only one person, according to the law of justice. But Jesus was more than human; He was divine. Also, through Him, humanity was created. That is why only His life could be offered as a sacrifice worthy of atonement for all humankind.

He offered for sin (see Isaiah 53:5, 6, and 10) His wealth of life that more than equaled the accumulative wealth of the lives of all human beings. Yet it was a conditional offering.

The Condition for Our Salvation

People must place their faith in the finished work of Christ and repent of their sin. Thus they receive the salvation that frees them from Satan as taught by judgment-conviction. By refusing to accept God's will, people submit to the lordship of Satan (see John 8:44) and thus forfeit the hope provided by the judgment of Satan. And by not going wholeheartedly for God they open their hearts to become encumbered with the weeds of materialistic hope—that which is earthly—the cares of this life and /or the deceitfulness of riches. They are sold on the supposed value of the material rather than being sold on God and committed to the life they can have in Him.

Certainly no one can have faith in Jesus for salvation who willfully persists on the very course from which Jesus died to save him. Salvation is more than an act of divine forgiveness by which a person can claim salvation from eternal damnation. Salvation also involves turning from sinful practices in this life, to "work out your own salvation" through obedience to God (see Philippians 2:12).

Therefore, to disobey God voluntarily is to reject the life that God provides and to demonstrate lack of hope in the very salvation that a person claims. Furthermore, if one truly repents, he abhors sin (see Romans 12:9) and looks to Jesus to save him from sin (see Matthew 1:21). This doesn't mean that a person is saved from eternal damnation by works or a life style (see Ephesians 2:8). People receive the gift of salvation through faith alone. But this faith will be demonstrated in the works that follow the change of heart that this faith brings. And works do have something to do with that aspect of salvation that enhances life here on earth. Works enable Christians to be the salt of the earth (Matt. 5:13) and to influence the wicked to become righteous. Also, works have a lot to do with keeping Christians in the relationship with God that keeps their faith for salvation intact. Faith comes only from a relationship with God, so if relationship with God is broken, faith no longer exists.

In connection with Satan's judgment at Calvary, the Holy Spirit, through judgment-conviction, teaches a dual truth. First, those who "neglect so great a salvation" (see Hebrews 2:3) will receive punishment and eternal death along with Satan. Second, when people trust Christ's finished work at Calvary, their sins "precede them unto judgment" (see 1 Timothy 5:24). This means that their sins are judged to be

Hope Fulfilled

forgiven at this time so that these saved ones do not have to worry about facing judgment for their sins when they die. This is the positive side of judgment-conviction. Therefore, judgment involves both reward for the righteous and punishment for the wicked. Paul highlights the dual truth of judgment that will render to each one according to his deeds and eternal life to those who by patient continuance in doing good seek for glory, honor, and immortality. But to those who are self-seeking and do not obey the truth but obey unrighteousness, indignation and wrath, tribulation and anguish, come upon every soul of man who does evil (see Romans 2:6-9a).

Satan has lost the hold he had on God's people through death and Hades. We read, "O Death, where is your sting? O Hades, where is your victory?" (1 Cor.15:55). And, "I am He who lives, and was dead, and behold, I am alive forevermore. Amen. And I have the keys of Hades and of Death" (Rev. 1:18).

Hades is the place where the unconverted go. Christ conquered death by dying in our place. In so doing, He defeated the power of death and Hades. As a result, God's people no longer go to Hades, as the Old Testament people did. The righteous Old Testament people who went to Hades (Sheol) were released by the conquest Christ made to be with Him in heaven.

Judgment-conviction directs the conscience for spiritual hope in Christ's judgment of sin and Satan. This hope is in opposition to the weeds of earthly, materialistic hope that tend to grow in the heart's soil. The effect of hope in Christ's offering is felt in the conscience, "For if the blood of bulls and goats and the ashes of a heifer, sprinkling the unclean, sanctifies for the purifying of the flesh, how much more shall the blood of Christ, who through the eternal Spirit offered

Himself without spot to God, cleanse your conscience from dead works to serve the living God?" (Heb. 9:13–14).

Sin-conviction, by producing understanding of the wickedness of sin, causes the intellect to have a profound sense of guilt that cultivates it for placing faith in the mercy of God.

Righteousness-conviction, by a spiritual beholding of Jesus, causes great love for Jesus and His character. This cultivates the will to have a strong aspiration to be like Jesus —like Him in righteousness.

Judgment-conviction produces a keen sense of the inestimable value of Christ's atonement on the cross. This cultivates the conscience to place hope in Christ's finished work and cleanses it from empty hope.

God has provided an outpouring of the Holy Spirit on the heart's soil. The Spirit sows the gospel seed and cultivates the heart soil through conviction, but He also saturates the hearts of people with His presence as rivers of living water. Naturally speaking, water is necessary to produce growth in plants. Likewise, the Spirit's presence is necessary to have spiritual life and growth.

> On the last day, that great day of the feast, Jesus stood and cried out, saying, "If anyone thirsts, let him come to Me and drink. He who believes in Me, as the Scripture has said, out of his heart will flow rivers of living water." But this He spoke concerning the Spirit, whom those believing in Him would receive; for the Holy Spirit was not yet given, because Jesus was not yet glorified (John 7:37–39).

John baptized people with water signifying that they had repented, but John also declared that one coming after him, referring to Jesus, would baptize people with the Spirit (see Matthew 3:11; Mark 1:8; Luke 3:16; John 1:33). A baptism is a total immersion, so John was looking forward to a time when people could be totally immersed in the Spirit. The prophets prophesied of this New Testament phenomenon:

> For I will pour water on him who is thirsty, And floods on the dry ground; I will pour My Spirit on your descendants, And My blessing on your offspring" (Isa. 44:3).
>
> And it shall come to pass afterward That I will pour out My Spirit on all flesh; Your sons and your daughters shall prophesy, Your old men shall dream dreams, Your young men shall see visions. And also on My menservants and on My maidservants I will pour out My Spirit in those days (Joel 2:28–29).
>
> But this is what was spoken by the prophet Joel: And it shall come to pass in the last days, says God, That I will pour out of My Spirit on all flesh; Your sons and your daughters shall prophesy, Your young men shall see visions, Your old men shall dream dreams (Acts 2:16–17).

Those who first received this outpouring of the Spirit in the upper room on the first day of Pentecost (see Acts 2) experienced the influence of the Spirit in developing a relationship with Jesus. But, with this outpouring, their relationship with God took on the vitality and power of the life that Jesus died to give. This was a higher level of living than they had ever known before. Instead of being vacillating and self-seeking, they became bold in united effort to fearlessly proclaim Jesus with a resolve that they had never known before. As a result, thousands of others were brought to faith in Christ for salvation on that very day.

Many people in the Old Testament experienced power from the Spirit. But normally the Spirit just came upon them rather than completely taking possession of them. In New Testament times we are commanded to be filled with the Spirit (see Ephesians 5:18), and it is stated that this filling, or outpouring, happened on the Day of Pentecost (see Acts 2:1–4). The Greek word for filled literally means to be "crammed." The soil of the heart is to be "crammed" with the Spirit. This is living life to the fullest. It is through the Spirit's outpouring that abundant life is generated in heart's soil:

> Now hope does not disappoint, because the love of God has been poured out in our hearts by the Holy Spirit who was given to us (Rom. 5:5).
>
> And if Christ is in you, the body is dead because of sin, but the Spirit is life because of righteousness. But if the Spirit of Him who raised Jesus from the dead dwells in you, He who raised Christ from the dead will also give life to your mortal bodies through His Spirit who dwells in you (Rom. 8:10–11).
>
> Who also made us sufficient as ministers of the new covenant, not of the letter but of the Spirit; for the letter kills, but the Spirit gives life (2 Cor. 3:6).
>
> It is the Spirit who gives life; the flesh profits nothing. The words that I speak to you are spirit, and they are life. (John 6:63).
>
> For he who sows to his flesh will of the flesh reap corruption, but he who sows to the Spirit will of the Spirit reap everlasting life (Gal. 6:8).
>
> And the Spirit and the bride say, "Come!" And let him who hears say, "Come!" And let him who thirsts come. Whoever desires, let him take the water of life freely (Rev. 22:17, NKJV 2004 edition).

The metaphor "soil," representing the heart in relationship to the metaphor "rain," representing the coming of the Spirit, presents an important picture of the Spirit entering the Christian's life. Soil can receive rain, becoming moist—"pour water on Him who is thirsty." It can also become saturated or "crammed" with water—"floods upon the dry ground" (see

Isaiah 44:3). The Holy Spirit wants to fill the thirsty heart to the extent that the entire soul is immersed or baptized. In this manner the Holy Spirit takes full possession of the Christian.

Spirit baptism starts by the washing of regeneration as the sprinkling of rain, but that is not enough; the heart, mind, and entire soul need to be saturated with the water of the Holy Spirit in entire, or complete, sanctification. From this point there is need of continual baptism to keep one cleansed of wrong propensities on the one hand and flooded with God's influence on the other. As fresh baptism keeps flowing, the Christian's capacity for more water of the Spirit increases. This hope of the outpouring of the Spirit also fills the heart with the love of God that incorporates faith and hope, as we see in Scripture: "Now hope does not disappoint, because the love of God has been poured out in our hearts by the Holy Spirit who was given to us" (Rom. 5:5). In this baptism the Spirit purifies the heart from the self-centeredness, which is sin, to God- centeredness.

W. T. Purkiser indicates that the baptism of the Spirit has not been clearly identified theologically with entire sanctification and that the question of the relation is still open.[44] This is largely because original sin has been viewed, more or less, as a foreign agent that in and of itself is a nature that pollutes the human nature. With this understanding, the work of sanctification must be viewed as a process of eradicating that foreign agent. However, when we view original sin as natural, normal drives and passions being perverted by self-centeredness, it can readily be seen that when God becomes central, the perversion or twist in the nature is corrected. The orientation of the drives and passions

---

[44] WT Purkiser, *Exploring Christian Holiness* (Kansas City: Beacon Hill Press), 108, 109 & 114.

begins to shift to God as the Holy Spirit's influence is realized in justification. Then, through Christian growth, the shift continues and finally becomes fully centralized on God through the dominance of Spirit baptism. Thus the baptism of the Spirit, by its nature, purifies the heart of humanistic, sensualistic, materialistic self-centeredness, and this process is the very essence of entire sanctification. By recognizing this, we clearly see how the baptism of the Spirit is related to entire sanctification. The baptism of the Spirit is the very essence of entire sanctification.

Jesus in Relation to the Holy Spirit

The Bible shows that both Jesus and the Spirit are in the Christian. What is the role of each and how do these roles relate to each other? In a certain sense, Jesus has gone from the world (see John 16:7), yet in another sense, He abides with the Christian (John 15:5). He said, as recorded in John 6:56, "He who eats My flesh and drinks My blood abides in Me, and I in him."

We partake of His flesh and blood by learning of Him and believing in Him. This involves accepting the truth of the Bible along with trusting Him as Savior and yielding to His Lordship. In this feeding on Jesus (see John 6:57), our personalities take on the image of Christ, or Christian character. In short, He abides in us as the truth and grace of God.

However, Jesus is not the actuator of the communion that we experience with God. This communion is actualized in the person of the Spirit. Stated another way, the communion we experience with Jesus and the Father takes place in the person of the Holy Spirit. Also, we could accurately say that it is the

Spirit's voice we hear when we are communing with God. In turn, the Spirit communicates our prayers to God as they need to be prayed to make them effective (see Romans 8:26).

The hope of the faithful people of the Old Testament, and others, for victory over sin's dominion, has been fulfilled at its highest level in the person of the Holy Spirit. Thus the life that Jesus died to give people is fully realized only through life in the Spirit.

The Holy Spirit is able to penetrate the inner person of every believer because He is not limited by time and space. He cultivates the intellect with the plow of sin-conviction. He cultivates the will with the plow of righteousness-conviction; and He cultivates the conscience with the plow of judgmentconviction. Thus the wayside soil, the stony soil, and the thorny soil of the heart are cultivated into good soil by these plows of conviction.

As a believer progressively yields to God, the Holy Spirit progressively fills that person's heart until a full surrender to Him occurs. At this stage one's heart, mind, and entire soul become fully saturated and crammed with the Holy Spirit, who then increases the individual's capacity for more water of the Spirit.

The highest level of hope is fulfilled in the Holy Spirit. This is not to say that He is more the God of hope than He is the God of faith and love. But, as we have been observing, hope is the product of faith through love. In fact, all of the three dynamics are present in each of the three respective dispensations of each member of the Godhead. The difference is in the emphasis.

In the Father's dispensation, faith was emphasized. In the Son's, a high level of emphasis on love was added. In the Holy Spirit's dispensation, all the hope of God's salvation promises is fulfilled. And this hope is the result of faith having come to maturity in the collective conscience of God's people through the power of Christlike love. This faith-maturity was especially present in the disciples who first received the baptism in the upper room.

The hope fulfilled in the Holy Spirit restores the instinctive value-judgment of the conscience into the good soil of finding inestimable value in Jesus and the life He provides. Therefore, truth in the form of hope causes the heart to answer the question, "Where should I focus my capacity for hope?" The heart answers with a keen sense of the value to be found in God, "Plug your hope into Jesus and the abundant life He gives."

Hope Fulfilled

Plows Representing Holy Spirit Conviction and Rain Representing the Outpouring of the Holy Spirit Added to Agricultural Picture of Conquering the World

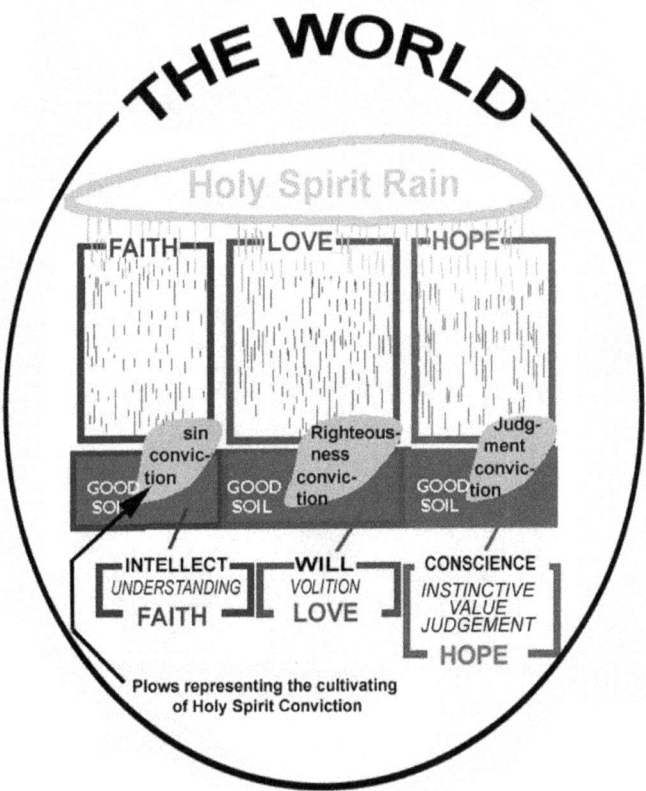

Plugged-in to the Dynamic Word

CHAPTER 8 The Spiritual Dynamics of Attitude

The angle of an airplane, up or down in relation to the wind it encounters, is called attitude, and it is one of the primary factors that make an airplane fly. The attitude must be properly adjusted to experience lift. Likewise, certain attitudes play a significant part in lifting people above spiritual defeat.

Each of the Beatitudes relates directly to Christian development. The first three are primarily about faith development. The second three are primarily about love development. The third three are primarily about hope development. Hence the Beatitudes point to the means of rising into the blue skies of spiritual conquest. They also demonstrate how the Holy Spirit breaks up the soil of the heart in greater detail than we have heretofore considered. In this chapter we learn what attitudes we should adopt to become spiritual conquerors.

The First Three Beatitudes Show Faith Development

Jesus said, "Blessed are the poor in spirit, for theirs is the kingdom of heaven" (see Matthew 5:3). A poor-in-spirit person has a great sense of his spiritual need, just as a person who is poor, materially speaking, has a great sense of his material need, especially when he beholds those who are wealthy. With this sense of spiritual poverty, the wayside-soilheart (Matt. 13:4), hardened in self-reliant pride, begins to soften. As long as one's intellect remains "hardened in pride" (Dan. 5:20), his intellect remains hardened against understanding that he is spiritually in poverty. But a poorinspirit attitude causes one to realize that he is not self-sufficient, and this understanding begins the breaking up of the fallow ground of his intellect (see Jeremiah 4:3). With this breaking up comes faith, for faith is trust in God or God-reliance as opposed to the self-reliance of pride. In Thayer's Greek Lexicon, pride is referred to as "an insolent and empty assurance, which trusts in its own power and resources and shamefully despises and violates divine laws and human rights."[45]

Faith is the cutting edge of sin-conviction. It cuts away at pride until self-reliance gives way to receiving the seeds of God-reliance in heart soil. If one is already a Christian, he is poor in spirit in that he knows he needs more of God. He recognizes that great spiritual wealth is available to him. Awareness of spiritual poverty lays the groundwork for faith to tap the spiritual wealth of the kingdom of heaven ("For theirs is kingdom of heaven").

Next Jesus said, "Blessed are those who mourn, for they shall be comforted" (Matt. 5:4). Mourning for sins committed is a normal expression of the poor-in-spirit attitude. As a person's sense of need relative to sin increases, his heart gives way to deep, sorrowful mourning. This is not a case of casual concern, but rather deep penitence for having sinned against God. Such mourning is the result of serious self-inspection that finds the sinner in want. His mourning conditions him to turn from his own ways to faith in God's way. The apostle Paul wrote, "For godly sorrow produces repentance leading to salvation, not to be regretted; but the sorrow of the world produces death" (2 Cor. 7:10 NKJV, 2004 edition).

---

[45] *Thayer's Greek Lexicon*-Online Bible (Bronson, Michigan: Online Bible U.S.A., 1955).

Accordingly, this sorrow is not one of despair, but rather a sorrow of faith that is focused on the Man of Sorrows, acquainted with grief (see Isaiah 53:3). The mourner is due to receive the faith-understanding that God forgives and is thereby comforted. If one is already a believer, he has a strong tendency to mourn over others' needs for which he finds comfort in prayer ("For they shall be comforted").

Jesus next taught, "Blessed are the meek, for they shall inherit the earth" (Matt. 5:5). Meekness is further evidence of the hard heart becoming softened. This opens understanding to the gospel seed (see Matthew 13:4), allowing it to penetrate deeply into the heart soil with the message of confession and humble trust, "God be merciful to me a sinner" (Luke 18:13). Then, as confession is made, faith trusts Jesus as Savior and Lord, causing the gospel seed to germinate into a relationship with God. This faith relationship is confirmed in the witness it bears by the Spirit of God (see Romans 8:16; 1 John 5:10). Thus "full assurance of faith" in God for justification is born (see Hebrews 10:22).

Repentance, by its nature, is an act of faith. Why? Repentance is a rejection of faith in Satan's ways and a turning to faith in God and His ways. Thus by nature it is faith in God. Repentance is the flip side of the coin of faith. We cannot have faith without repentance.

Meekness opens the heart's door to Christ (see Revelation 3:20), and with Christ comes all that He left in His will (see Ephesians 1:9-12) for His people to inherit (see Galatians 4:7; Revelation 21:7), including the future renovated earth. A meek Christian spirit also has the tendency to disarm people's resistance to God, giving a very effective edge in promoting God's cause on the earth ("For they shall inherit the earth").

Meekness, like all other Christian character developments in the Beatitudes, continues to grow in the life of the believer. One should keep in mind that the sequence of spiritual growth we see in these Beatitudes is primarily a cause-effect sequence that does not necessarily include a time sequence.

The Second Three Beatitudes Show Love Development

The Lord continued, "Blessed are those who hunger and thirst for righteousness, for they shall be filled" (Matt. 5:6). The love of God (*agape*) expresses itself in spiritual hunger and thirst. This strong desire strengthens the will. How? Strong desire builds an intense determination to obtain its object, and this growing determination is the will being strengthened. Regeneration plants a desire for righteousness in the heart. "Therefore, if anyone is in Christ, he is a new creation; old things have passed away; behold, all things have become new" (2 Cor. 5:17).

The new convert has a healthy appetite for righteousness, just as a new baby has a healthy appetite for food. Humankind lost inner righteousness in the Edenic fall, but hunger and thirst for righteousness is a desire for the restoration of inner righteousness.

The hunger and thirst for the love of God is contrary to the pull of alien love that Paul describes: "For what I am doing, I do not understand. For what I will to do, that I do not practice; but what I hate, that I do" (Rom. 7: 15). Paul is describing the tendency of the heart apart from the dominant influence of the Spirit. Obviously, he is not describing his personal life after his conversion, for he declares, "I have lived in all good conscience before God until this day" (Acts 23:1).

"The rabbis, the Jewish teachers of ancient times, often used this first-person style to convey truths universally valid."[46] Paul was writing in this style, so the "I" in Romans 7:15 is the typical person who is trying to live right apart from salvation grace. Under these circumstances, such a person commits overt sinful acts while struggling with a desire to do otherwise. Justified Christian people may not sin, yet some remaining pull of alien love for sin may still reside in their hearts after they have been justified.

The stony nature of wrong desire (see Ezekiel 11:19; 36:26) resists the deeper growth of the roots of Christian character in heart soil as we see in the parable of the sower (Matt. 13:3–9, 20–21). This weakens the will toward righteousness. Yet, those who develop a hunger and thirst for righteousness through the love of God will be filled with righteousness ("For they shall be filled").

Jesus continued His teaching by saying, "Blessed are the merciful, for they shall obtain mercy" (Matt. 5:7). Offering mercy is focused on others and their concerns, including God's concerns. It reaches out to others. This means it is opposite in nature to the stony resistance to God that is composed of selfcentered desires, or lusts that disregard others. Therefore, it tends to cultivate any remains of these lusts from the believer's heart, such as, "adultery, fornication, uncleanness, lewdness, idolatry, sorcery, hatred, contentions, jealousies, outbursts of wrath, selfish ambitions, dissensions, heresies, envy, murders, drunkenness, revelries, and the like" (see Galatians. 5:19–21). Being merciful struggles against these impulses of the lust of the flesh-sensualism.

---

[46] *Wesley Bible* (Nashville: Thomas Nelson Pub. 1990), page 16929, comment on Romans 7:14

A merciful person will not be inclined to commit adultery and fornication because he realizes that they hurt others. Showing mercy is not compatible with idolatry because idolatry is basically worshiping self and taking care of self at the expense of ignoring the interests of others. A merciful person will not be inclined to be jealous because he is glad that others have things that bring them pleasure, even if he does not have them himself. He will not be selfishly ambitious and envious. Drunkenness and revelries trample on the rights of others, so these are not compatible with being merciful. A merciful person certainly will not have the resentments that cause dissensions and murder. Being merciful cries for strength to reject any elements of those tendencies that may yet remain after Jesus comes to live in the heart. Showing mercy is the very heartthrob of God (see Exodus 34:6). It is the motivation in His desire to redeem us. It is interesting to note that the mercy beatitude is the central one of the nine Beatitudes. This is fitting because God's entire salvation program rotates around the axis of mercy. By its very nature, mercy wins the favor of God and others and thus inclines believers to return the same ("For they shall obtain mercy").

Jesus told His disciples and us, "Blessed are the pure in heart, for they shall see God" (Matt, 5: 8). As our hungering and thirsting for righteousness gradually increases, it is understandable that the heart could come to a crisis. This would be a crisis of remaining love for sin warring against the love of God that is being developed by our hungering and thirsting for righteousness. This becomes a confrontation between these opposing love forces on the battleground of the will. It is also understandable that this battle would lead to the death of one of the two love forces. This battle is what caused the stony heart in the parable of the sower to stumble. It was the death of his shallow love for God. He developed no root of godly love. Therefore, his relationship with God endured only for a while. "But he who received the seed on stony places, this is he who hears the word and immediately receives it with joy; yet he has no root in himself, but endures only for a while. For when tribulation or persecution arises because of the word, immediately he stumbles" (Matt. 13:20–21).

However, God intends for His people to win the battle against sin. Therefore, it is understandable that a time would come when the love of God would finally destroy the remaining stony resistance to God as it continues to call for the death of all that is contrary to God.

The Result of the First Five Beatitudes

The first five beatitudes focus on attitudes. Then, abruptly, the sixth beatitude turns the focus to a condition of the heart that by its nature shows itself to be the result of proper attitudes. The poor-in-spirit awareness of spiritual poverty (first beatitude), in sorrowful repentance (second beatitude), with teachable openness to God (third beatitude), is clear evidence that faith for trusting Jesus as Savior is being developed. Thus, the first three beatitudes show attitudes leading to justification. And justification brings a person into contact with Jesus so that the beholding of righteousness in Him through Spirit conviction can begin (see John 16:7–11).

Consequently, it is understandable that the love received from this process would create the hunger and thirst of the fourth beatitude and the mercy showing of the fifth beatitude. Then, having developed these basic five attitudes that have the collective attitude of disdaining the self-centeredness of sin, the Christian would naturally be crying out for the pure heart of the sixth beatitude.

Therefore if any remaining sinful desire should be detected, it would be expected that the heart would experience an exceedingly strong desire to have it removed. In this frame of mind, it is understandable that a person could consecrate himself to God more fully than would have been possible when he first came to Jesus for salvation.

When we first come to Christ we are more conscious of the guilt of our committed sins and their consequences than anything else. Therefore our main concern is what Jesus can do for us. But after one has had time to develop appreciation for Jesus and His program of bringing others to righteousness, the concern tends to be more of the question of what can I do to help promote this worthy program and further identify with it. Such a full-surrender commitment offers one's self as a "living sacrifice" (see Romans 12:1) and acquires faith for a pure heart (see Acts 15:9). We understand that a pure heart has been cleansed of love for sin and is full of the love of God.

Thus this heart is undividedly committed to God and the truth.

The believer is one who wants to have an undivided heart. In Ezekiel 11:19–20, "one heart" suggests singleness of heart, or an undivided heart, as a basis for great rapport between God and His people. (The New International Version of the Bible says that this is an "undivided heart.") Such a heart is not divided between godly love and sinful love. Therefore it is perfected in love, as John describes.

> No one has seen God at any time. If we love one another, God abides in us, and His love has been perfected in us. By this we know that we abide in Him, and He in us, because He has given us of His Spirit. And we have seen and testify that the Father has sent the Son as Savior of the world. Whoever confesses that Jesus is the Son of God, God abides in him, and he in God. And we have known and believed the love that God has for us. God is love, and he who abides in love

abides in God and God in him. Love has been perfected among us in this: that we may have boldness in the day of judgment; because as He is, so are we in this world. There is no fear in love; but perfect love casts out fear, because fear involves torment. But he who fears has not been made perfect in love. We love Him because He first loved us (1 John 4:12–19).

John clearly implies that no one has seen God apart from love and that we see God through the love of God that has been perfected in us. How does love enable us to see God?

Perfected (purified) hearts are filled with the love of God in undivided commitment to Him. This love gives the follower of Jesus rapport with God because this love senses that all condemnation and rejection has been removed from the relationship a believer has with God. Thus the relationship becomes transparent, with no barrier of guilt to obscure the beholding of Jesus. Jesus is clearly seen in all the beauty of His righteous character ("For they shall see God"). This is also why those perfected in love have boldness toward God. "There is no fear in love" (1John 4:18).

The statement, "Pursue peace with all people, and holiness, without which no one will see the Lord" (Heb. 12:14), has the same significance. Both references point to the love relationship seen in 1 John 4.

Does heart purity and perfect love have a bearing on seeing God in eternity? Of course it does; but the prerequisite for seeing God, as we read in 1 Corinthians 13:12, is an intimate love relationship with God. "I shall know just as I also am known" happens "when that which is perfect has come" (1 Cor.13:10)—when love has been perfected. The whole thirteenth chapter of First Corinthians is about love; it is not about heaven. Therefore, this passage is describing a transparent love relationship that can be perfected here and now. Call it entire sanctification (see 1 Thessalonians 5:23), call it perfect love (see 1 John 4:18), call it heart purity (see Matthew 5:8); they all express the love for God that the sixth beatitude promises will cause people to see God ("For they shall see God").

The Third Three Beatitudes Show Hope Development

Jesus said, "Blessed are the peacemakers, for they shall be called sons of God" (Matt. 5:9). Scripture shows us, "For to be carnally minded is death, but to be spiritually minded is life and peace" (Rom. 8:6). Peace comes to those who are spiritually minded as a result of being perfected in love because perfect love cleanses them of the carnal mind, the selfcentered perspective that destroys peace. When this peace comes, it provides the life filled with hope that God intended for His people. The God of peace, who is also the life, provides this sanctified life. "Now may the God of peace Himself sanctify you completely; and may your whole spirit, soul, and body be preserved blameless at the coming of our Lord Jesus Christ. He who calls you is faithful, who also will do it" (1 Thess. 5:23–24).

As the God of peace leads people out of the darkness and turmoil of Satan's grip to the peace of God, they become peacemakers. For the peace they experience, combined with God's love, causes them to want to lead others to this peace. The hope within this God-given peace gives the positive mental attitude necessary to sell Jesus to the world.

Then, as God's people succeed in this type of peacemaking, they see lives changed from the ruin and dysfunction of sin to the hopeful life in Christ. This gives such joy and inspiration that winning people to the peace of Christ becomes the Christian's consuming passion. This gives Christians a unity of purpose that tends to remove any

The Spiritual Dynamics of Attitude

infighting or disunity so that they end up experiencing the making of peace among themselves.

The sum result of Christians leading people out of the darkness and confusion of sin into the hopeful life of the peace of Christ and generally promoting peace causes them to be recognized as the children of God, because God is the God of peace ("for they shall be called sons of God").

We have been told by Jesus, "Blessed are those who are persecuted for righteousness' sake, for theirs is the kingdom of heaven" (Matt. 5:10). One of the paradoxes of God's spiritual economy is that persecution, by which Satan intends to discourage, produces hope instead. Paul links tribulation, which includes persecution, with hope: "And not only that, but we also glory in tribulations, knowing that tribulation produces perseverance; and perseverance, character; and character, hope" (Rom. 5:3–4).

History proves that persecution produces strong character. God's people could face with rejoicing even the wild animals that tore them to shreds. Persecution has a way of focusing our minds on spiritual conquest. It is a type of spiritual challenge that builds determination to persevere, and perseverance builds Christian character. As a result, Christians receive the spiritually healthy, God-centered and God-dependent selfconfidence that is hope.

This hope is the essence of what fulfills the promise of this beatitude. It gives Christians the incentive to prevail in the matter of building the kingdom of heaven ("For theirs is the kingdom of heaven"). They shall also be "counted worthy of the kingdom of God" (2 Thess. 1:5) through enduring persecution.

Our Lord continued His teaching with the words, "Blessed are you when they revile and persecute you, and say all kinds of evil against you falsely for my sake" (Matt. 5:11). Slander is a form of persecution, so most of what was said about the eighth beatitude applies here. Slander may destroy a reputation, but it has a way of reminding Christians that their hope is based on a personal relationship with Jesus rather than on the respect that others have for them. Therefore, slander can program the conscience to place greater value on a relationship with God as it reveals the uncertainty of a relationship with others that is often based on reputation. Slander may be the ultimate challenge to Christian character.

However, persecution could very well be God's method of freeing the conscience from the powerful peer pressure that enslaves so many of us. This pressure has the tendency to make us more emotionally bonded to our peers than to God. While slander may take more grace to endure than any other trial or persecution, the reward for enduring it is great ("For great is your reward in heaven").

Faith, love, and hope cause the attitudes and conditions of the Beatitudes. Yet the three also grow out of the Beatitudes, reversing them from causes to effects. Thus, faith causes one to be poor in spirit, and the poor-in-spirit attitude produces faith in the spiritual wealth of Jesus and His way. Also, faith in Christ's way, causing one to mourn over one's sinfulness and to thus mourn, produces faith in Him who is sinless. Furthermore, faith develops meekness, and meekness opens one's heart soil to receiving more faith.

The love of God possesses a hunger for righteousness, and such hunger beholds Jesus with the effect of producing more love. Love produces mercy, and the exercise of showing mercy increases love. Love produces a pure heart, and a pure heart grows in love for God and fellow humans.

Hope in God's program gives us inspiration for winning people to His peace, and this peacemaking builds hope in His program. Hope in God may bring on persecution, but persecution can solidify and grow hope in God. Hope can also bring on slander, but slander can strengthen hope in God.

We recognize that all of the Beatitudes relate to faith, love, and hope. Yet it is our contention that the first three relate mostly to faith, the second three relate mostly to love, and the last three relate mostly to hope.

The Beatitudes are an expression of basic Christian exercise, faith prevailing in its process of producing hope through love. Collectively, the Beatitudes portray the progressive sanctifying effects of love with faith and hope incorporated. The former is the triad being acted out by people; the latter is the triad acting in people to sanctify them wholly, entirely, or completely.

In the overall picture of heart cultivation, the spiritual dynamics of the Beatitudes can be viewed as wheat plants that grow in the good soil of a proper relationship with God. Thus the Word in the form of attitude continues to grow in our hearts with its empowering effects. Again we emphasize, we do not study the Bible just to satisfy our curiosity or to be fascinated with its uniqueness. We study God's word to apply its truth to our lives with its life giving vitality. As we study the Bible, especially as we study it holistically, we plug-in to the Holy Spirit and the love He pours out in our hearts, because the Spirit lives in the Word. This love fills us with the excitement of experiencing God and His power working in us and through us.

Plugged-in to the Dynamic Word

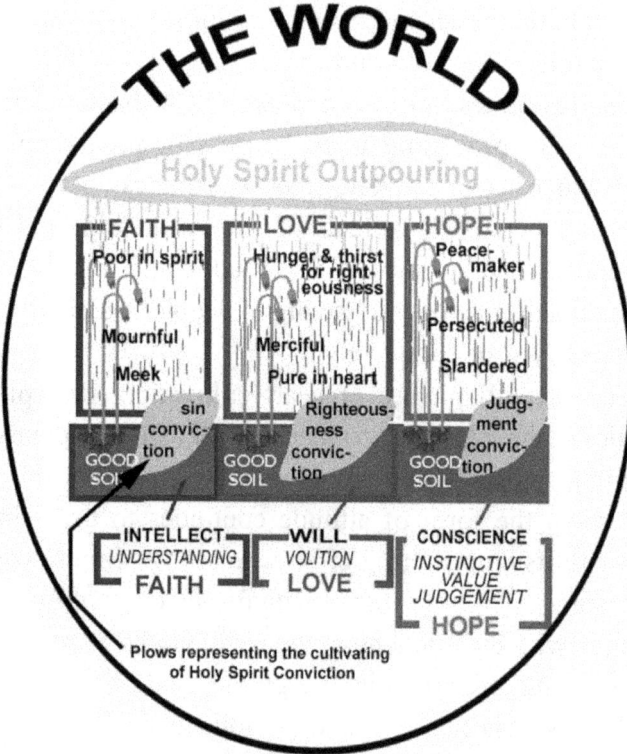

Wheat Plants Representing the Qualities of Christian Character Development Added to Agricultural Picture of Conquering the World

CHAPTER 9 The Fruit of the Spirit

The farmer works and sweats to plow, plant, and cultivate. He prays for rain and sunshine while his heart fills with expectation. When plants grow from the seed and fruit finally appears and ripens in abundance, he reaps his award with great joy. Although living for God gives us personal benefits far beyond what living for self gives, our greatest motivation should be to please God. His joy is to see our lives bear fruit that reflects His image restored in us.

We have examined the causes of spiritual unproductiveness which we have identified as selfcenteredness expressed in humanism, sensualism, and materialism. We have observed that humanism (perverted faith) and materialism (perverted hope) are expressions of sensualism (perverted love). In other words, sensualism incorporates humanism and materialism to produce the works of the flesh. Sensualism is the core.

Conversely, in much the same pattern, love, incorporating faith and hope, sanctifies the personality toward God and away from the self-centeredness of evil. Love is the core. As people become more and more God-centered, the fruit of the Spirit replaces the works of the flesh. This fruit is contrasted with the works of the flesh in the Bible:

> Now the works of the flesh are evident, which are: adultery, fornication, uncleanness, lewdness, idolatry, sorcery, hatred, contentions, jealousies, outbursts of wrath, selfish ambitions, dissensions, heresies, envy, murders, drunkenness, revelries, and the like; of which I

tell you beforehand, just as I also told you in time past, that those who practice such things will not inherit the kingdom of God (Gal. 5:19–21, NKJV 2004 edition). But the fruit of the Spirit is love, joy, peace, longsuffering, kindness, goodness, faithfulness, gentleness, self-control. Against such there is no law. And those who are Christ's have crucified the flesh with its passions and desires. If we live in the Spirit, let us also walk in the Spirit (Gal. 5:22–25).

Love, Joy, and Peace—the Fruit of Faith

Love finds its roots in faith, for the belief one places in God becomes the soil for God to plant love. It is a love that is built on the determination to act in character with God's will. Love grows with the developing belief that comes as faith matures (see the definition of faith in chapter 2). Therefore, love empowers one to choose to trust as belief comes to maturity. In this capacity, love is the fruit of faith.

Joy also finds its roots in faith, for joy comes from the assurance of salvation found in faith. Paul speaks to the Philippians of their "progress and joy of faith" (see Philippians 1:25). Lack of joy normally indicates lack of faith. When the joy bells of heaven quit ringing in the heart, it is time to take spiritual inventory; we need to repent and pray until the faith that produced that joy is restored. The "joy of the LORD is your strength" (Neh. 8:10). It is one of the most distinguishing traits of the Christian life.

Peace comes from faith, by the fact that faith trusts in God, and trust produces a rest that is the result of ceasing humanistic works (see Hebrews 4:10). This rest is the essence of peace.

Love, joy, and peace are fundamentally rooted in faith and dependent mostly on faith. Although all three also involve love and hope (obviously love does), it seems that they are basically rooted in faith and are therefore largely the fruit of faith.

Longsuffering, Kindness and Goodness—the Fruit of Love Some versions of the Bible translate the word "longsuffering" as patience; if we put these words together we get the fuller meaning, which is patient longsuffering. This quality seems to find its roots primarily in love. Elements of faith and hope play their part in longsuffering, but love must be the greatest source of patient longsuffering. Love "suffers long" (see 1 Corinthians 13:4). Kindness is not superficial; it involves moral goodness. Unbelievers expect this from Christians more than any other virtue. It dramatically shows the love of Christ to a lost world. This fifth quality of the fruit of the Spirit is closely related to mercy, spoken of in the fifth beatitude. Both are central in their respective categories. Love not only "suffers long," it is "kind" and "does not behave rudely" (see 1 Corinthians 13:5).

Goodness involves uprightness and generosity, and it holds the qualities of love. Love "does not seek its own, is not provoked, thinks no evil" (1 Cor. 13:5). It is very obvious that goodness is an expression of love. Where goodness is lacking, more love is needed. The common ontology of longsuffering, kindness, and goodness is love. They are perhaps the strongest expressions of the love of God. Therefore, they are largely the fruit of love. They are rooted in love.

Faithfulness, Gentleness, and Self-control—Fruit of Hope

Faithfulness indicates reliability. It results from having the hope that does not disappoint (see Romans 5:5), for this hope causes one to rely on God which, in turn, tends to make the person reliable. This phenomenon is seen in Philippians 3:14, "I press toward the goal for the prize of the upward call of God in Christ Jesus." The hope of the prize keeps one pressing on and produces spiritual achievers. If a servant loses the hope of his master's return, he will tend to become careless and unfaithful (see Matthew 24:48-49).

Gentleness is a quality of mildness, as opposed to harshness and roughness. A hopeful spirit tends to be gentle rather than demanding in harshness and roughness. This attitude hopes in God so, therefore, it does not need to place its hope in the opposite, which is self-centered demeanor. When a servant wickedly loses hope that his master is returning he may tend to be harsh with others (see Matthew 24:48-49).

Self-control is the last fruit mentioned and may be the ultimate achievement of hope in this life. One loses control along with hope when he gives in to his selfish drives and passions, but he gains self-control when he accepts the discipline of a godly life. In this discipline one discovers the foundation for self-control, and in this he has hope.

The last three qualities of the fruit of the Spirit (faithfulness, gentleness, and self-control) are largely expressions of hope in God for ourselves and others—"hope that does not disappoint" (see Romans 5:5). Therefore, they are rooted in hope.

The fruit of the Spirit is generalized in Ephesians 5 as goodness, righteousness, and truth, in connection with the command to "walk as children of light" (see Ephesians 5:8).

This "walk," illuminated by God's "light," is the self-control that keeps God's people in the truth pattern of producing the

The Fruit of the Spirit

fruit of the Spirit rather than the "unfruitful works of darkness."

> Therefore do not be partakers with them. For you were once darkness, but now you are light in the Lord. Walk as children of light (for the fruit of the Spirit is in all goodness, righteousness, and truth), finding out what is acceptable to the Lord. And have no fellowship with the unfruitful works of darkness, but rather expose them. For it is shameful even to speak of those things which are done by them in secret (Eph. 5:7–12, NKJV 2004 edition).

As with the Beatitudes, it seems that the nine components of the fruit of the Spirit are purposely presented in an order that can be divided into three triads in relation to faith, love, and hope. The first triad, which is love, joy, and peace, is rooted in faith. The second triad is longsuffering, kindness, and goodness, which is rooted in love. And the third triad, which is faithfulness, gentleness, and self-control, is rooted in hope. All of these qualities, operating as a unit, are expressions of faith prevailing in its process of producing hope through love.

To help us conceptualize how the fruit of the Spirit relates to the spiritual conquest accomplished in heart cultivation, we view this fruit as being produced in heart soil. It is the fruit that is brought forth, some a hundredfold, some sixty, some thirty through being plugged-in to the vitality of the Word (see Matthew 13:23). May we concentrate on studying the Bible holistically to have a greater flow of this vitality. By thus abiding in Jesus, His words will abide in us and bear much

Plugged-in to the Dynamic Word

fruit (see John 15:7, 8). Of course we cannot expect to live holy lives apart from the empowerment of the Word and the Holy Spirit. We must be plugged-in to the Word and be baptized with the Holy Spirit to bare the fruit of Christlike character.

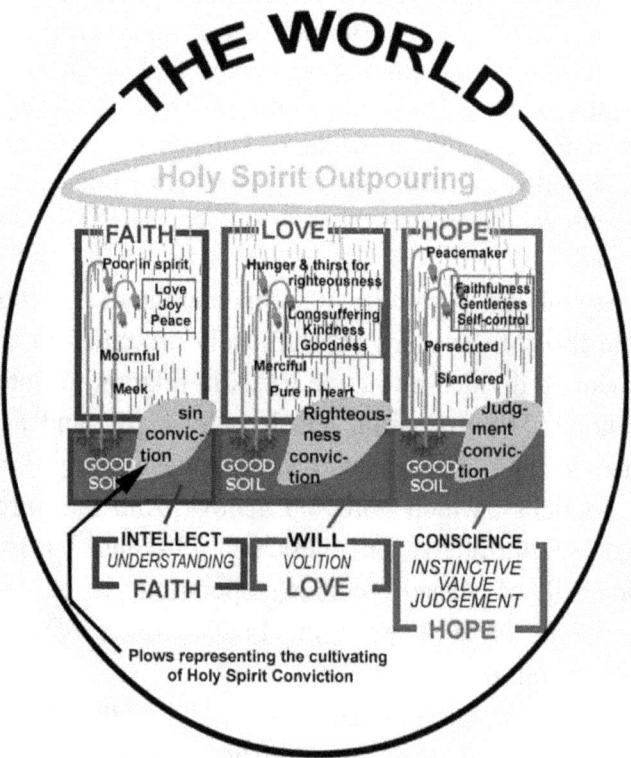

The Fruit of the Spirit, Represented as the Wheat of the Wheat Plants, Added to Agricultural Picture of Conquering the World

CHAPTER 10 The Triads Blended Express Faith, Love, and Hope

Spiritual development is a triune process in terms of faith, love, and hope in various forms. Now it is time to further test the findings of our study by assembling all of the triads we have found in Scripture. Some of these, we have found, are specifically named in the Bible. Others we have found there by theological deductive reasoning. If all of these truly play a vital part in building Christian character to restore the image of God in fallen people, they should interactively blend together to show a united picture of grace applying truth to lives. First we will list the triads and then we will blend them. There are two lists, one that reflects the order of developing relationship with God and one that shows the order of Satan breaking down relationship with God.

List of Triads that Reflect the Order of Developing Relationship with God

1. The faculties of the heart: intellect, will, and conscience
2. The capacities of the heart faculties: understanding, volition, and value-judgment
3. The three types of conviction: sin-conviction, righteousness-conviction, and judgment-conviction
4. The triad with which Jesus identifies Himself: the way, the truth, and the life
5. The three phases of truth: truth-revelation, truth-reality, and truth-functionality

6. The unproductive soils of the parable of the sower: the wayside soil, the stony soil, and the thorny soil
7. The problems of the three soils: hardness, weak will, and poor sense of value
8. The triad of triads in the Beatitudes. The first three beatitudes: awareness of spiritual poverty, in mournful penitence, and meek openness to God. The second three: hunger and thirst for righteousness, producing mercy and heart purity. The last three: enthusiastic peacemaking in spite of persecution and slander
9. The triad of triads in the list of the fruit of the Spirit: love, joy, peace; longsuffering, kindness, goodness; faithfulness, gentleness, self-control

The first element of each of these triads is involved in the development of faith, the second element of each triad is involved in the development of love, and the third element of each triad is involved in the development of hope. This sequential order reflects the fact that relationship with God starts with faith, builds through love, and ultimately produces hope.

List of Triads that Reflect the Order of Satan Breaking down Relationship with God

1. The spiritual dynamics of Satan's kingdom: the lust of the flesh, the lust of the eyes, and the pride of life
2. The temptations to lust presented to Eve: tree was good for food, tree was pleasant to the eyes, tree was desirable to make one wise
3. The temptations to lust presented to Jesus: command this stone to become bread, the devil showed all the kingdoms,

throw yourself down from here

Satan has a clever process of breaking down Christian character and relationship with God. First, he tries to pervert our love for God into the lust of the flesh so that our resolve to maintain relationship with God is weakened. Second, he tries to pervert our hope in God into the lust of the eyes so that we see less value in God. Third, he deals the death blow by perverting our faith into the pride of life. Satan knows that by destroying our faith-dependency on God with prideful dependency on self, he destroys the dynamic through which we are saved. For it is by grace we are saved though faith (see Eph 2:8).

Development of Faith, Love, and Hope

Man's basic problem is his sin problem. Jesus implied that sin is a faith-related problem. A faith understanding is produced in the intellect through sin conviction of our spiritual poverty apart from God and His grace that is available for our sin need. Understanding our sin need and God's promise relative to that need teaches us the basics of depending on God for all needs: "By faith we understand" (see Hebrews 11:3). This understanding has an orientation to God's way as opposed to man's way. In fact, the faith dynamic is directly integrated with the way. And the way is the revealed way of truth. It is truth revealed.

The pervered-faith pride of life-humanism is the primary enemy of faith. It causes people to be self-reliant as opposed to being God-reliant. The hard wayside soil in the parable of the sower depicts the heart's hardening against God caused by pride. The first three beatitudes show the heart being cultivated from the hardheaded, closed-minded, proud intellect to a meek openness to God that penitently mourns its spiritual poverty.

This opens the door of the heart to Jesus, effecting justification, regeneration, and our adoption into the family of God. This begins the process of producing the fruit of the Spirit, especially the first three qualities—love, joy, and peace—for they are primarily the fruit of faith because they are largely rooted in faith.

The essence of sin is self-centeredness, and Jesus implied that this depravity is a love-related problem in stating the reason for righteousness-conviction, "I go to My Father and you see Me no more." The Holy Spirit enables us to behold Jesus through righteousness-conviction since we cannot see Jesus physically, as the disciples did while He was on this earth. (This idea was developed in chapter 7.) This beholding causes us to love Him in all of the beauty of His righteous character and in so doing acquire into our hearts the love of God that loves what God loves and hates what He hates. The love of God, so acquired, is desire for holiness by which the will is strengthened to consistently choose righteousness. This love is directly integrated with the truth, for the truth is God's love answer to the truth of our need.

The perverted-love lust of the flesh-sensualism, being rooted in self-love, is the primary enemy of love. It is sensual love resisting the love of God. The good soil on top of the hard stone-pan of the stony soil, referred to in the parable of the sower, depicts the weak will toward God resulting from the shallow love of those not yet entirely sanctified. The second three beatitudes show the process of love being developed in the form of a hunger and thirst for righteousness which produces God-centered mercifulness. A hunger and thirst for righteousness, along with mercy, cultivates the self-centered resistance to God from the heart, resulting in heart purity—being perfected in love. The second three qualities of the fruit of the Spirit—longsuffering, kindness, and goodness—are largely the fruit of love, for they are rooted in love. These are perhaps the strongest expressions of the love of God.

The conscience is programmed to truly value the spiritual above all else by a type of hope that comes from the realization of value in that which pertains to building and establishing God's eternal kingdom. Through this process the conscience develops proper value judgment. This hope relates to the fact that "the ruler of this world is judged," Jesus' stated reason for judgment-conviction (see John 12:31). The judgment of Satan is the basis of our hope to overcome him in his attempts to send us to the punishment of judgment and also the basis for our hope to have our sins judged now, to be forgiven, that we might reap the rewards of eternal life—the life that God gives to the forgiven. Judgment-conviction teaches us the inestimable value of Christ's atonement in accomplishing all of this. Hope is faith having laid hold of a specific promise from God, and all God's promises are based on the hope incorporated in judgment-conviction. Hope is directly integrated with this life that Jesus offers—the life He refers to in saying I am the way, the truth and the *life*, because the life is hope-being-realized.

The perverted-hope lust of the eyes, being earthly and materialistic, is the main enemy of this hope that finds value in God. The thorny soil of the parable of the sower depicts a value system that finds more value in giving attention to the "cares of this world" and "riches" than in being a part of God's kingdom. The thorns or weeds depict materialistic enthusiasm crowding out the good plants of enthusiasm for God. The last three beatitudes show the weeds of materialistic hope being cultivated from the heart through the enthusiasm produced by the hope of being delivered from the confusion and turmoil of

The Triads Blended Express Faith, Love, and Hope

sin into the peace of God. This peace becomes the foundation and incentive for becoming peacemakers, especially in the matter of leading others into the peace of God. And the enthusiastic hope produced by peacemaking is increased by persecution and slander, as has been demonstrated in Christian martyrdom. (This idea was developed in chapter 8.) The last three qualities of the fruit of the Spirit: faithfulness, gentleness, and self-control, are largely the fruit of hope in God for ourselves and for others—"hope that does not disappoint" (see Romans 5:5).

Faith is developing belief in God, formed in the intellect that matures into the choice of the will to trust in God. It is God-reliance as opposed to self-reliance that diminishes or excludes trust in God. Love, referring to the love of God, is distinguishable from mere human love. It is God's nature made known in Christ that loves what God loves and hates what He hates and thus is determined to act in character with God's will.

Love is the understanding of God's nature made known in Christ. It is from this revelatory perspective that we come to know love as unmotivated and unmanipulated, unconditional and unlimited. Such love is not a matter of feeling, which cannot be commanded in any case, but of commitment and action. It is at the farthest pole from sentimentality and is related to the Old Testament word for "covenant love" or "steadfast love" (*hesed*).[47]

---

[47] *The New Interpreter's Bible,* vol. 8 (Nashville: Abingdon Press, 1969), 425.

Hope is faith having laid hold of a specific promise of God. Or, stated another way, it is faith trusting God to fulfill a specific promise that He has made. It is also an appraisal of value in God formed in the conscience deeming God desirable and trustworthy.

Three Dynamics

Basic Christian exercise is faith prevailing in its process of producing hope through love. And that sanctification happens in love with faith and hope incorporated. The three dynamics work in unison. However, while love expresses itself in faith and hope, love is a reality that in and of itself is more than the sum total of faith and hope. This can be illustrated with colors. Let us think of faith as blue, love as purple, and hope as red. Purple is made up of blue and red. Therefore, it cannot exist apart from these colors, but the interaction of red and blue causes a completely different color to come forth. The purple that results is a separate entity. However, it can then be placed with red and blue to provide a color combination that is much more beautiful than any one or two that the colors make by themselves.

These three colors were used in the tabernacle where spectacular beauty was required. Accordingly, if faith, love, and hope could be represented with these colors, they could illustrate the spectacular spiritual beauty that results. Faith and hope are beautiful components of love, as blue and red are the same of purple. But in the interaction of faith and hope, love simultaneously comes forth in even greater beauty than either faith or hope possess individually. Love is the greatest and most beautiful of all three, as purple was by far the most expensive and valuable of any of the fabrics in Bible times.

The Triads Blended Express Faith, Love, and Hope

Let us recap on how the triad begins in Christians. The Word of God enters the intellect in a dormant, seed-like state. With this comes belief and, as belief matures, the will exercises it into trust. As trust happens, the hope and love of the Word of God become active. Now the three begin the basic Christian exercise of faith prevailing in its process of producing hope through love. This is the triad being acted out by people, which immediately causes the triad to begin acting in people to sanctify them wholly, entirely, or completely—the sanctifying process of love incorporating faith and hope. Thus sanctification begins in the new birth of the Christian's life and eventually leads to a full surrender to God which further enhances the ongoing sanctifying process.

Faith, love, and hope are constantly acting in harmonious conjunction with the operation of the other two. With this understood, look at the interaction of the three faculties of the heart in conjunction with the interaction of faith, love, and hope.

The understanding of the intellect and the values of the conscience are expressed in the will's choices. So when the intellect is not properly informed by faith, and the conscience is not properly programmed by hope, the love capacity of the will is shallow and weak. Under these conditions, the will lacks determination to continually seek after God. On the other hand, if faith and hope are strongly in place, with faith adequately informing the intellect and hope adequately programming the conscience, love produces a strong determination of the will to seek God and serve Him fervently.

Conversely, the same is true with the spiritual processes of the devil's kingdom. Really, the pride of life is perverted faith, the lust of the flesh is perverted love, and the lust of the eyes is perverted hope. Thus the pride of life and the lust of the eyes are expressed in the lust of the flesh. Accordingly, the pride of life informs the intellect with humanism and the lust of the eyes programs the conscience with materialism. And humanism and materialism find expression in the will in the form of sensual passion influencing choice to reject God and rebel against Him.

The spiritual processes of Christ's kingdom and Satan's kingdom are thus basically narrowed down to the spiritual warfare of the love of God versus the love of the world. This is the core issue of spiritual conquest that takes place on the battleground of the heart.

"Love Divine by Charles Wesley

Charles Wesley's song "Love Divine" sounds forth the magnificence of the love of God. By "Love divine, all loves excelling," Wesley means that the love of God excels over all the loves of the world:

> Love divine, all loves excelling,
> Joy of heaven, to earth come
> down; Fix in us thy humble
> dwelling; All thy faithful mercies
> crown!
> Jesus, thou art all compassion,
> Pure, unbounded love thou art; Visit
> us with thy salvation;
> Enter every trembling heart.

Battle Hymn of the Kingdom of God

God's truth marching to the Holy Spirit's drumbeat of spiritual conquest through faith, love, and hope.

Theological Reconciliation

The focus on faith, love, and hope has the potential to bring some theological reconciliation among Christians who have become polarized on certain doctrinal issues. Serious Christians feel strongly about the tenets of their faith, so where there is disagreement, division arises. Yet many of us long for some basis for unity that does not compromise our faith.

Some have suggested that we can have unity by agreeing on the essentials and having charity toward one another on the issues that are nonessential. That sounds good, but the problem is that few of us believe that any of our tenets are nonessential. Therefore, this idea doesn't bring us one iota closer to unity.

The only basis for unity among serious Christians is truth. We all agree that we must uncompromisingly hold to the truth even though we may have disagreement on what truth is. We agree that we must hold to truth and that we cannot sacrifice it on the altar of unity.

We do agree on many basic issues. For example, all Biblebelieving Christians agree that salvation comes by grace through faith in Jesus Christ. We believe in the virgin birth of Jesus, and so on. But disagreement arises on the provisions of Christ's atonement, the work of the Holy Spirit, how we show our faith by our works. Then, as we each defend our positions, we tend to become more entrenched. This often leads to polarization and more disunity. What really is tragic is that Satan takes advantage of the situation to influence some to view those who disagree with them as enemies of the cross.

If we would all focus more on developing our relationship with God, we would also develop a stronger heart-to-heart relationship with each other. This rapport would make us more inclined to try to understand each other's views. As we try, we might find that some of our disagreement lies in terms and semantics. In areas of real disagreement, we would desire to learn from each other's perspectives. With this blending of the minds we would also be more likely to focus on areas of agreement rather than on our disagreements and thus develop greater unity. This approach does not call for unity at the sacrifice of truth. Instead, it calls for unity on the basis of a deeper understanding of truth.

The development of faith, love, and hope helps us build our relationship with God and thus could help us come together. Also, the study of this triad is a focus on basic truth that could give us the common ground for the agreement that we have suggested. Furthermore, the study and development of this triad in our lives should help us acquire a passion to live out one of the most important truths of the Word. This truth is that our discipleship to Christ is demonstrated by our obvious love for one another (see John 13:35).

About the Author

Larry Grabill has pastored and guided people to the Lord since 1982 in the United States and Nigeria. Through phone, post mail, and email he mentored a Bible School in Calabar, Nigeria, that he helped start from 1994 to 2004 where he served as a resident missionary from December 1992 to December 1993. (This Bible School is now indigenous.) He received his ministerial training from God's Bible School in Cincinnati, Ohio.

The author's four children are fervent Christians whose households are fully dedicated to God. One son pastors the largest church of his denomination, another, who has been a successful custom home builder, is now studying to be Medical Doctor. Both daughters work in the medical field. One is a nurse manager. Larry's intense interest in God is shared by his twelve grandchildren.

Larry has also written *Things Come Together*, a romance novel from African culture showing African tribes coming together in Christian unity to greatly improve society. Written with two Nigerian authors, it is a response to *Things Fall Apart*, a sad tale of greedy, arrogant colonial powers clashing with African religion, fear, and pride to the devastation of society. This book has been recommended for all of the junior secondary schools of Cross River State by the state's Ministry of Education.

Things Come Together is based on the theology and thought form set forth in *"Plugged-in to the Dynamic Word: Living in Faith, Love, and Hope"*

www.ingramcontent.com/pod-product-compliance
Lightning Source LLC
Chambersburg PA
CBHW061324040426
42444CB00011B/2767